Math for the Anxious

Math for the Anxious
Building Basic Skills

Rosanne Proga

Boston   Burr Ridge, IL   Dubuque, IA   Madison, WI   New York   San Francisco   St. Louis
Bangkok   Bogotá   Caracas   Kuala Lumpur   Lisbon   London   Madrid   Mexico City
Milan   Montreal   New Delhi   Santiago   Seoul   Singapore   Sydney   Taipei   Toronto

The McGraw·Hill Companies

Higher Education

MATH FOR THE ANXIOUS: BUILDING BASIC SKILLS

1 2 3 4 5 6 7 8 9 0 DOC/DOC 0 9 8 7 6 5 4 3

ISBN 0–07–288584–X

Publisher, mathematics and statistics: *William K. Barter*
Publisher developmental mathematics: *Elizabeth J. Haefele*
Director of development: *David Dietz*
Senior developmental editor: *Randy Welch*
Senior marketing manager: *Mary K. Kittell*
Lead project manager: *Susan J. Brusch*
Production supervisor: *Sherry L. Kane*
Designer: *Rick D. Noel*
Cover designer: *Lindsey Huber*
Cover image: *©Getty Images, Victoria Falls, Zimbabwe, #DV802077*
Compositor: *The GTS Companies/York, PA Campus*
Typeface: *10.5/12 Times*
Printer: *R. R. Donnelley Crawfordsville, IN*

Library of Congress Cataloging-in-Publication Data
Proga, Rosanne.
    Math for the anxious : building basic skills / Rosanne Proga. — 1st ed.
        p. cm.
    Includes index.
    ISBN 0–07–288584–X
1. Mathematics—Popular works. I. Title.
QA93.P76   2005
510—dc22   2003065154
                                            CIP

www.mhhe.com

To All My Teachers

CONTENTS

CHAPTER 8
Succeeding with Signed Numbers   103

CHAPTER 9
Mastering Measurement   115

PREFACE

Math for the Anxious: Building Basic Skills is intended to provide a practical approach to the problem of math anxiety. Even though we live in a technological age filled with computers, fax machines, and cellular phones, most adults are intimidated by the prospect of having to use the mathematical concepts that make our modern innovations possible. Many adults are paralyzed by their inability to do math. It may manifest itself in the embarrassment of not being able to figure out how many gallons of paint are needed to paint a room, or how much flour is needed to bake a double batch of cookies. It may also restrict your career possibilities if you need mathematical skills to further your education or to advance to a more challenging position. Our lack of confidence in dealing with numbers may even affect our ability to make informed decisions regarding the kinds of leaders we should elect to guide us through the new century.

Throughout my years teaching mathematics, I came to realize that many students were not aware of the study skills that can make the difference between being successful in math and being totally confused by the subject. Many of the strategies discussed in this book for overcoming math anxiety resulted from discussions with students who had problems learning mathematics—particularly those returning to study the subject after a long time with no exposure to mathematics courses. Some techniques may seem like common sense to you, and you may be using them already. Others will require some discipline to make them a part of your study habits. Probably, not every idea I present will be useful to you, and it is up to you to decide which techniques work best for you. Every student is different, and a strategy that is very helpful to one person may not benefit another.

FEATURES

Icons designate the recurring features of this book:

 Math Memories introduce each chapter and are based on the actual experiences of students who have had prior difficulties learning math so that readers will realize they are not alone and that their challenges in math are surmountable.

 Common Problems discuss frequently occurring obstacles and explain why each topic is difficult to learn.

 Hints for Studying each topic are designed to assist readers in mastering mathematical concepts.

Strategies for Success highlight the building blocks for achieving proficiency in each newly acquired skill by summarizing key concepts.

 Exercises at the end of each chapter provide opportunities for students to reinforce their understanding. To obtain the greatest benefit, some may done as a group activity or with an experienced teacher or tutor.

Other innovative features include

- An emphasis on **understanding *why*** a technique is used to solve a problem to reduce the need to memorize rules.
- A presentation of a **stepwise approach to problem solving** to build confidence in one's ability to do math.
- **Clear definitions** of mathematical terms to make the subject accessible to readers of all skill levels.
- **Well-organized lists** that summarize mathematical procedures and make it easy for readers to look up how to solve a problem.
- A **focus on estimation** so that students can simplify calculations, check the accuracy of their work, and make fewer mistakes.
- An abundant use of **diagrams** to illustrate mathematical principles.
- **Practical examples** that illustrate how mathematics can be applied to daily living situations.

To obtain the maximum benefit from reading this book, you might find it helpful to use it in conjunction with a textbook. The chapters that address specific mathematical concepts, such as fractions, decimals, percents, and geometry, are meant to give a basic overview rather than to substitute for a complete explanation of the topic. It is important that you have a textbook available that presents each topic in a thorough and well-organized fashion, including a complete index that makes it easy for you to look up concepts that you have trouble understanding. Textbooks generally provide a well-thought-out development of all the mathematical concepts in a particular subject area. This book differs from a textbook in that it provides a greater in-depth discussion of selected mathematical topics that are particularly troublesome for many students.

By reading this book, you are taking the first step toward becoming less math-anxious. As you apply the techniques discussed here to your study of mathematics, you will eventually reach a point where you notice that you actually *enjoy* doing math. Savor your feelings of success when you are able to get the right answer, or when you are able to help someone else work through a math problem. The analytical approach to problem solving that you acquire while studying mathematics can help you tackle new problems that arise in daily living situations. Soon your successes will begin to outnumber your failures, and you will no longer feel disabled by your mathematical deficiencies.

You will begin to reap the benefits of a newly found confidence in yourself and in your own abilities. As with anything else in life, the beauty of mathematics can only be appreciated by those who have the courage to look at it with open eyes.

ACKNOWLEDGMENTS

I would like to thank all the people who contributed to the development of this book. I am especially grateful to the following reviewers for their helpful comments. In particular, I would like to extend my thanks to Stacy Shoemake, a student at Drury University, for reading the entire manuscript and commenting on it from a student's perspective.

Gerald Busald, *San Antonio College*

Elizabeth Condon, *Owens Community College*

Cynthia Craig, *Augusta State University*

Beth Fraser, *Middlesex Community College*

Jacqueline Giles, *Houston Community College–Central*

Rosalie Hojegian, *Passaic County Community College*

Mary M. Leeseberg, *Manatee Community College*

Rodolfo Maglio, *Oakton Community College*

Jean Millen, *Georgia Perimeter College*

Fred Peskoff, *Borough of Manhattan Community College/CUNY*

Mary Romans, *Kent State University*

Elizabeth Russell, *Glendale Community College*

Lisa Sheppard, *Lorain County Community College*

Stacy Shoemake (student), *Drury University*

Bryan Stewart, *Tarrant County College*

Abolhassan Taghavy, *Richard J. Daley College*

Alexis Thurman, *County College of Morris*

I wish to express my sincere gratitude to all my teachers who have helped me learn and grow throughout my life. I have had the tremendous good fortune of benefiting from their wisdom and guidance. The students I have worked with over the years have helped me to maintain a high level of enthusiasm for teaching mathematics and have challenged me to always provide clear and thorough explanations of mathematical concepts. The editors and staff at McGraw-Hill have helped produce a text that presents the material in a style that is well-organized and easy to follow. In particular I would like to thank David Deitz, Director of Development, for having the vision to see the need for this book; Randy Welch, Senior Developmental Editor, for providing many helpful suggestions; Mary Kittell, Senior Marketing Manager; Susan Brusch, Lead Project Manager; Rick Noel, Designer; Sherry Kane,

Production Supervisor; and Rick Meisner for checking the entire book for accuracy.

I would like to thank my father for continuing to be a source of inspiration to me and helping the project move ahead by remembering to ask, "How's the book going?" My friends and family have all patiently listened to me discuss my ideas for this book, and encouraged me to continue writing. Finally, I would like to express my heartfelt appreciation to Peter Marzuk for his ongoing support and understanding. His insightful feedback and delightful sense of humor over the years have been critical to the completion of this book.

Rosanne Proga

The Misery of Math Anxiety

MATH MEMORIES

"I have struggled with understanding math ever since early childhood. I avoided taking math courses whenever I could, and now I am prevented from furthering my education and changing careers."

"I failed every math course in high school, so every year I had to go to summer school, just because I could not do math."

"My lack of understanding of math really holds me back in the business world, since it takes me so much longer to get an answer, or I don't get one at all."

"The invention of the calculator has been my only saving grace in the workplace, because without it, I cannot do even the simplest calculations. My goal is to be able to do math without a calculator."

"I just bought a computer and I need to learn how to complete worksheets. However, without understanding math, I cannot fill in the formulas correctly."

"I never took a math course in college, but now I teach grammar school and I need to be able to explain math to children. I want to develop confidence in my ability to understand math so that I don't confuse my students in the same way my teachers confused me."

MATH ANXIETY: WHAT CAUSES IT?

Much has been written in the past few years on the problem of math anxiety. The term has been used to describe a variety of symptoms that can result from an emotional reaction, a skill deficiency, or a combination of both.

Math anxiety is usually evidenced by an inability to use mathematics in daily living situations. It is often characterized by an avoidance of any task requiring the use of even the simplest mathematical techniques, such as figuring out a tip in a restaurant, or balancing a checkbook. It sometimes carries over into other tasks that require some form of mechanical aptitude or intense concentration. Many people who have math anxiety avoid doing such things as reading road maps, or following the instructions necessary to program a VCR, to operate a camera, or even to play a board game. Some math-anxious students have a deep-rooted fear of never being able to understand, much less master, even the simplest mathematical techniques. They try to conceal their ignorance from others because of fear of embarrassment, and this often enhances their anxiety.

It is important to examine some of the causes of math anxiety, to determine how to overcome the obstacles that prevent math-anxious individuals from advancing their knowledge of mathematics. Most students who have great difficulty with mathematics suffer from a series of repeated failures and frustrations, which eventually convince them that they can never do math. Many people recall experiences in grammar school when the teacher demanded a correct answer that they were unable to produce, and as a result, they suffered the consequences of punishment, embarrassment, or bad grades. Others can trace back to the point when they first had trouble understanding a particular concept, after which time it was all downhill. Many times this difficulty can be attributed to skipping some material covered in a math class because of changing schools, switching classes, or illness. Unfortunately, the mental blocks can sometimes begin to form as a result of poor teaching at some point in a student's mathematical education. Occasionally, elementary school teachers are not prepared to teach mathematics and would prefer not to do so. They may convey their own anxiety to their students by giving unclear explanations and displaying an unwillingness or inability to respond to questions. In high school and college, many math teachers who are highly skilled in mathematics are unable to teach at their students' level of understanding. The students who cannot grasp the material presented attribute their difficulties to their own inability rather than to a teaching deficiency.

You might be asking why this situation would have such a profound impact on a person's mathematical ability, while similar problems encountered in other academic disciplines, such as English or history, do not seem to have such lasting consequences. One reason is that mathematics is a cumulative body of knowledge. A mental block in learning a particular skill encountered in grammar school will inhibit a student's understanding whenever that skill is required to master another mathematical technique. Until that roadblock is removed by teaching the student the basic concept he or she does not understand, the student may never feel completely capable of learning the new material presented in a math class. Usually, once we have completed a certain level of mathematical education in grammar school or even high school, we do not get an opportunity to repeat the material, unless we flunk the course.

Another difference between mathematics and other academic disciplines is that mathematics is a skill that must be practiced. Learning mathematics is more like learning to play a musical instrument than learning history. The concepts presented by a teacher who is working out problems at the board in front of the class cannot be thoroughly mastered until they are practiced by the student. In addition, lack of continuous practice causes the skill to be easily lost. Learning math is not simply a matter of memorizing the steps needed to solve a problem. It requires that you practice each newly acquired skill until using it becomes automatic. Many math-anxious students have gaps in their mathematical training because they were not required to take a math course to complete their educational program. In addition, most people do not have an encyclopedia of mathematics at home where they can look up how to do calculations they have forgotten, such as calculating a percent or multiplying fractions. A book such as this, or any textbook in basic mathematics, can be used to look up mathematical procedures when you cannot remember what to do.

The notation and vocabulary of mathematics are very precise and technical. Students unfamiliar with particular words and symbols may be confused or even intimidated. Words such as *and, or, point, slope, prime, real, imaginary, rational, irrational, differentiate,* and *integrate* have very specific meanings in mathematics that differ from their everyday usage. In addition, mathematical symbols may have more than one meaning, and some mathematical concepts can be expressed by using many different notations.

For all these reasons, many students believe in a popular myth that one needs a "math mind" to feel comfortable with mathematics. The challenge to all students and teachers involved in the study of mathematics is to dispel this myth. The strength of our society, given the demands of living in a technological age, will depend on it.

TO SUCCEED IN MATH . . .

Many people who suffer from math anxiety have many mistaken ideas as to what is needed to succeed in math. These misconceptions create mental obstacles that prevent a math-anxious adult from developing his or her own abilities to their fullest potential. Despite what you might think about people who are "good at math," each of the following statements is actually true.

To Succeed in Math . . .

1. You do not need to be born with a special ability.
2. You do not need to think that math is easy.
3. You do not need to be perfect.
4. You do not need to know immediately how to get the right answer.
5. You do not need to know the one best way to solve a problem.
6. You do not need to do problems very quickly.
7. You do not need to do complicated calculations in your head.
8. You do not need to remember everything.

We will now examine each of these in greater detail.

To Succeed in Math You Do Not Need to Be Born with a Special Ability

There have been many gifted individuals throughout history who have excelled in a variety of fields, including music, art, literature, science, mathematics, and others. The degree to which their remarkable achievements can be attributed to an inborn talent will continue to be widely debated. However, this does not preclude the fact that people of average intelligence can learn to play a musical instrument, draw a picture, write a story, understand science, or master basic mathematics. The level of mathematical ability needed in daily life does not require the intellect of a genius. You do not need to be born with a "math mind" in order to learn how to work with fractions, decimals, and percents. As with any other learning, those who find math to be especially difficult may need to apply more time and effort to learning the subject.

To Succeed in Math You Do Not Need to Think that Math Is Easy

Many children who like mathematics and do well in math courses continue to study the subject in college and choose to pursue technical careers. These people may find everyday math very easy, partly because there was never any period of time when they were not using math. However, even these "mathematically oriented" people would probably admit to having at least one bad experience with math, such as a bad math teacher who was impossible to understand, or a difficult math problem that seemed impossible to solve. These experiences do not convince such persons that they cannot do math. Instead, they have enough confidence in their ability to continue to work hard to overcome any obstacles that confront them. It is also quite possible for a person who did poorly in mathematics as a child to gain the skill and confidence to master the subject as an adult. As long as you start from the beginning, you can learn enough math at almost any age to use it effectively in daily living situations.

To Succeed in Math You Do Not Need to Be Perfect

One of the main differences between people who are confident in their mathematical ability and those who are not is their attitude toward their mistakes, not whether they make them. By working slowly and carefully, you can reduce the possibility that you will make a mistake; but no one is always able to solve math problems perfectly every time. If you make a mistake, do not get discouraged or begin an internal dialogue that reinforces your belief that you will never be able to do well in math. Simply go back to the point in the problem where the error first occurred and try again. If necessary, you can always start over and work the problem through from the beginning. Remember that we all learn from our mistakes, and learning mathematics is no exception.

To Succeed in Math You Do Not Need to Know Immediately How to Get the Right Answer

Problem-solving skill involves using whatever knowledge you have at your disposal to arrive at a solution. The best way to solve a problem is to first eliminate possibilities that do not work. You may begin to solve a problem one way, only to discover that it does not lead to a solution. However, after a few "false starts" you will have more information to work with, and a method for finding the right answer may become more apparent. It is extremely important that you do not become impatient or anxious when a particular approach does not work. Putting pressure on yourself to get the right answer immediately simply creates stress and prevents you from thinking clearly. Thoughts such as "I will never be able to solve this problem" fuel negative emotions and take energy away from the logical thinking process. Those who are competent problem solvers do not become frustrated when their first attempt to find a solution does not lead to the answer. They regard this trial-and-error approach as a necessary process for solving many types of problems in mathematics.

To Succeed in Math You Do Not Need to Know the One Best Way to Solve a Problem

There are often many ways to solve a problem, and one way is not necessarily better than another. In fact, since different people find different methods easier to understand and use, there is no best way to solve a problem. Therefore, if you have difficulty learning a particular technique, you may benefit from trying another approach. If you think of a way to solve a problem that is different from the approach presented by a math teacher or a textbook, you may think that you must be doing something wrong. However, many problems can be solved by more than one method, and it is usually due to lack of time or space that alternative ways of solving the same problem are not presented.

To Succeed in Math You Do Not Need to Do Problems Very Quickly

The best way to avoid making careless mistakes when doing math is to work slowly and carefully, checking your work as you go along. Sometimes students are tempted to rush through a problem because they are afraid that they will forget what they are doing before they finish it. They may also be impatient and want to hurry up and get the answer in the back of the book. However, if speed causes you to make careless mistakes, it will take even longer to finish a problem than it would have if you had worked carefully from the beginning.

To Succeed in Math You Do Not Need to Do Complicated Calculations in Your Head

The most important abilities you can develop in order to be successful at math are your problem-solving skills. Being able to do complicated arithmetic or algebraic calculations in your head is not essential, especially in light of the prevalence of pocket calculators and computers. Also, if you do not write down every step of your solution to a problem and then do not get the right answer, it will be very difficult for you to go back and find out where you made a mistake. When you are taking a math test, it is especially important that you show all your work, because you may get partial credit for demonstrating that you know how to solve the problem, even if you get the wrong answer.

To Succeed in Math You Do Not Need to Remember Everything

Even the most brilliant mathematicians forget how to apply certain mathematical techniques if they do not use them for a long time. People who have a lot of difficulty with mathematics tend to avoid using math and therefore probably forget more than people who use math frequently. Given the appropriate amount of time, confidence, and effort, you can relearn any technique you cannot remember. If we forget how to spell a word, we simply look it up in a dictionary. If we forget how to get from one location to another, we ask someone for directions or look at a map. Unfortunately, since math reference books are not as readily available as dictionaries or road maps, people often attribute their inability to do math to their own deficiency rather than to a lack of accessible information.

WHY LEARN MATH?

As human beings, we all have a natural inquisitiveness and a desire to learn new things. Much of the time, the process of learning is so automatic that we are not even aware that it is happening. For example, if we go on vacation to a place that is unfamiliar to us, we quickly learn how to get to our hotel, where we can get something to eat, and the location of tourist sites we want to visit. We may get this information in a variety of ways, such as reading a guidebook, looking at a map, speaking to other people, or looking for landmarks as we walk down the street. If we are enjoying ourselves, learning may seem effortless; but if we encounter difficulties, learning may be regarded as a chore.

When we are having a good time while on vacation, we may be inspired to visit unfamiliar places, eat exotic kinds of food, interact with the people who live there, and embark on other new adventures. When it is time to go home, we are sad that the vacation is ending. We may even make plans to return to the same place on a future vacation. On the other hand, if we have bad weather, become ill, or encounter unfriendly people, we may be eager for our vacation to end. Once we return home, we vow never to go back to that place again.

Even when two people go to the same vacation spot, they may have such different experiences that it is hard to imagine that they visited the same place when you hear them talk about their trips. One person might say that the weather was perfect, the food was delicious, the people were wonderful, and there were lots of interesting things to do. The other person might say that the weather was awful, the food was nauseating, the people were rude, and there was nothing to do.

For many of us, our experiences in learning math have been worse than being on a bad vacation. We recall all the frustrating experiences we had trying to chart a course through unfamiliar territory that included fractions, decimals, percents, signed numbers, formulas, and equations. We had no guidebook to tell us where to go, we frequently got lost, and when we asked for help, we could not understand the directions and were ridiculed for being unable to follow them. At this point in our lives, it is difficult for us to understand how anyone can actually succeed in learning math, much less enjoy working out math problems.

We now need to lay the groundwork for taking a fresh approach to studying math. This begins with examining the past circumstances that surrounded our difficulties in trying to learn math in school. Some of us were criticized or ridiculed when we failed to keep up with the rest of the class and failed to make progress in our understanding of math. Others, responding to peer pressure, did not try hard enough because it was not "cool" to be a good math student. The by-product of these experiences is that they created obstacles to our learning, and sometimes they caused us to avoid math in order to avoid the negative feelings associated with the subject. It is well known that those who are rewarded for good work are motivated to keep trying to achieve higher goals, and those who are punished for doing poorly are more likely to develop anxiety and repeat their failures. Therefore, the successful math student is encouraged to master increasingly difficult concepts, while the unsuccessful math student continues to fall further behind.

It is important to be aware of your math history, but you must be willing to put it behind you. As adults, we need to reexamine our beliefs as to what it takes to learn math. We need to create the right circumstances that enable us to develop the conviction that we do indeed have the aptitude, motivation, and time to master the skills we need to acquire. Many of us feel that our failure to learn math is simply due to a lack of intelligence, a factor beyond our control. However, as discussed previously, the overwhelming majority of people do indeed have the ability to learn the basic math skills used in daily life.

In order to succeed, it is critical that we be aware of our personal reasons for wanting to study math. These must be strong enough to motivate us to overcome even the most difficult challenges we will face. Our goals now may be quite different from what they were when we were younger. We may have practical reasons for learning math—to complete a college degree, get a better job, or start a new career. We may also feel that the time has come for us to move beyond our past anxieties and to take on new intellectual challenges. If our motivation to learn math is weak, or if we do not see how it will help us to achieve our goals, we are undermining our efforts.

It is also important that we set goals for ourselves that are realistic and attainable, given the time we have available. Many students acknowledge that they would have done better in a math class if only they had had more time to study. Learning math is very time-consuming, because a lot of time is required outside of class for you to gain the skills you need to successfully solve problems. To develop self-confidence, you need to go beyond the point where a skill seems merely familiar to you, to where you have mastered it and feel that you can "do it in your sleep." If we are unable to schedule enough time to achieve that level of ability, then our understanding of math remains superficial and we will not have a solid foundation for learning more advanced concepts.

HOW WE LEARN MATH

We all use a variety of different ways to learn. These include observing, listening, and doing. For example, when we learned how to tie our shoes, we probably observed someone showing us how to do it. We also listened to that person explain each step of the process. The person teaching us may have even taken hold of our hands to guide us through the process of tying our own shoes. We use whatever means of learning are available to us simultaneously. For example, as we were trying to tie our own shoes, we carefully observed what we were doing and may have recited the steps we were trying to follow out loud or to ourselves mentally.

One of the most widely known models for describing how we learn is the *visual, auditory,* and *kinesthetic,* or VAK, learning style. It describes how we use our sense perceptions to gather information from our environment. We use the visual style when we learn by seeing, the auditory style when we learn by listening, and the kinesthetic style when we learn by doing. The word *kinesthetic* pertains to movement. As in the process of learning to tie our shoes, we often use a combination of all these styles to acquire a new skill. In a math class, we use the visual style as we watch the instructor write on the board, the auditory style as we listen to the verbal explanation, and the kinesthetic style as we take notes. In trying to solve a math problem, we proceed by reading the problem (visual), talking to ourselves in formulating a solution (auditory), and working out the steps with paper and pencil (kinesthetic).

If we examine our learning patterns, we may find that we prefer a particular style and find it easiest to learn when we use that style. For example, some students pay more attention to what the instructor is writing on the board, others prefer to listen to the explanation of the material that is being discussed, and still others focus on taking elaborate notes. This pattern may also vary depending upon the style of the instructor. Some instructors write a lot of notes on the board and say very little, while other instructors do just the opposite. Students who mostly stick to their preferred learning styles are at a disadvantage when it becomes necessary to use other styles when learning from a particular instructor. It is fine to be aware of your preferences, but be careful not to pigeonhole yourself as being a particular type of learner. Our learning preferences will change over time, and they need to change as we encounter different learning situations. We can all enhance our ability to learn math by trying a variety of techniques that correspond to a variety of different styles.

Other factors, such as our personality, have an important impact on how we learn best. Some students are outgoing and others are shy. Some students are risk takers and others are very cautious. Some prefer structure and others prefer flexibility. Not only is the list of variations endless, but also different personality traits become apparent in different situations. Our learning patterns are influenced by so many different factors, such as intellectual ability, personality, motivation, and past experience, that it is impossible to arrive at a perfect formula for success. However, the more we know about ourselves and the more we are willing to go beyond the imaginary limitations we set for ourselves, the more tools we will have to meet the challenges of learning in new situations.

PROBLEM SOLVING

Problem solving is the cornerstone for learning math. Generally, the most effective way to solve a problem is to apply a systematic approach that breaks the process down into a number of steps. We begin with defining the problem by identifying what we need to accomplish. We then collect and organize the information we have that will help us achieve our goal. Next we design a plan to follow that may lead to a solution. We execute this plan, which often involves using a process of trial and error. Finally, we analyze the result and determine whether we have indeed solved the problem or need to come up with a better strategy and start over. This process can be extremely complicated; but when we have a lot of experience in solving a particular kind of problem, we can apply these steps so quickly that the entire process seems effortless.

We use our problem-solving skills numerous times throughout the day to accomplish a variety of tasks that include ordinary activities such as getting to work, cooking a meal, or organizing a social event. However, if we are confronted with a problem that is unfamiliar to us, the process of trying to find a solution can be frustrating, overwhelming, and anxiety-producing.

A key point to realize is that problem solving is often a messy process that does not proceed in a predictable, orderly fashion. This fact is usually not obvious to us because of the way we are taught math. Math instructors, who are well prepared for class, use lecture notes that include complete solutions to problems, so they are unlikely to make many mistakes when working out those problems on the board in front of the class. Mathematics textbooks contain examples that only show you the correct solution, not all the wrong turns you might take in attempting to solve each problem.

The process of trial and error often involves making guesses, making mistakes, arriving at dead ends, and starting over. It takes a lot of confidence and motivation to stick with the process and not get discouraged. Often we are working out problems in isolation without the guidance of someone who has more experience and could help us determine which strategies are successful and which should be abandoned. We might make the mistake of repeating unsuccessful strategies that only add to our frustration and bring us no closer to a successful solution. However, the only way to really learn math is to practice solving problems again and again until we begin to recognize the patterns that lead directly to a solution. Learning any new skill may at first seem to be quite difficult and intimidating, but as human beings, we have an incredible capacity to perform many complicated tasks very quickly and automatically, once they are familiar to us.

At some point in the process, in spite of all our mistakes and false starts, things seem to fall into place and we feel that we finally "get it." Even though this flash of insight may seem to occur suddenly and without warning, it is actually the result of all our previous efforts in trying to solve the problem. We cannot force insight to happen, and we do not know how much time and energy it will take before we can savor its rewards. However, if we are patient and persistent, our hard work will pay off, and our sense of accomplishment will inspire us to strive for goals we never thought we were capable of attaining.

MATH ANXIETY: WHY MUST IT BE ADDRESSED?

As mathematics becomes an increasingly vital tool for survival in a technological society, more and more people who thought they could function without ever needing to use math are finding that this is impossible. This situation explains much of the recent emphasis on the problem of math anxiety.

Mathematics is being encountered with increasing frequency, and a lack of ability to cope with numbers can have a tremendously disabling effect on a person's life. Such a person is forced to rely on others, feels embarrassed by his or her incapacity, and lives in fear that his or her ignorance will be discovered. This feeling of being limited often carries over into other areas as well, such as reading detailed instructions or performing complicated tasks that require a lot of concentration.

Even while reading the newspaper, people are overwhelmed by numbers, charts, and graphs, and they often skip over them, missing the point that the author was trying to make. To become a critical reader, you must be able to understand the meaning and use of numbers. This is especially true of statistics, which are often used to mislead us into mistaking a theory for a fact.

We now live in a highly technological society, and we need informed citizens who will help make the decisions that will shape it. We cannot leave all the planning for the future to the experts. Their knowledge is often limited to their field of expertise, and it is tempting for them to act out of self-interest instead of considering the needs of society as a whole. We need responsibly educated laypeople who trust in their own abilities to intelligently consider the information provided by experts and to challenge the ideas that need to be questioned. We must demand that the experts help us attain the level of ability that will enable us to act in this regard.

It is also true that the careers that require some degree of mathematical ability are increasing in numbers. Your professional advancement may be halted, or your desire to switch careers may be beset by many limitations, if you are not comfortable with mathematics. Standardized tests, even for nontechnical fields, require some degree of mathematical competency. In addition, many fields of study that were once less mathematical, such as business and the social sciences, are now becoming very quantitative. The advent of widespread computer technology is beginning to make personal computers almost as common as television sets in many U.S. households. We must gain some degree of technical competence and confidence to be able to benefit from the advantages brought about by this new technology.

Finally, it is vital that we solve the problem of math anxiety so that we do not transmit our fears and insecurities to our children. If our society continues in the current direction, children will have to become even more adept at mathematics than we can possibly imagine now. We must demand that our schools provide them with high-quality instruction in mathematics, so that they will be prepared to handle the challenges that the future holds for them.

 ## STRATEGIES FOR SUCCESS

The key points you should remember to avoid the "misery of math anxiety" are summarized here:

STRATEGIES FOR SUCCESS IN MATHEMATICS

1. Convince yourself that you can learn enough math to cope with daily living situations.
2. Acknowledge that people can learn math at any age, even if they had great difficulty as children.
3. Do not get discouraged when you make mistakes.
4. Do not expect to solve every problem immediately. Use trial and error when necessary.
5. Remember that there is no one best way to solve a problem.
6. Work slowly and carefully, and check your work to catch careless mistakes.
7. Take a fresh approach and keep in mind your reasons for wanting to learn math.
8. Set goals that are realistic and attainable, given your available time.
9. Use a variety of techniques corresponding to different learning styles.
10. Develop strong problem-solving skills.
11. Look up mathematical techniques you have forgotten, and take the time to relearn them.

 ## CHAPTER I EXERCISES

1. Write a brief math autobiography. Describe your experiences with mathematics in grammar school, high school, and college. Try to include at least one positive experience you had when learning math. Also discuss how difficulties with mathematics might have influenced your choice of a major in school or your choice of a career.
2. Give at least two specific examples of how you use math or avoid using math in daily living situations.

3. Explain why you want to study math at this point in your life. What goals will learning math help you accomplish?

4. What techniques do you find to be most effective when you want to learn something new? Describe the combination of learning styles represented by each of these techniques.

5. Describe how you recently solved a difficult problem or performed a complicated task that was unrelated to math. What steps did you follow to break up the process? How did you feel when you became frustrated? How did you feel when you finally succeeded?

6. Describe three things you learned in this chapter that can help you reduce your math anxiety.

CHAPTER

2

Strategies for Conquering Math Anxiety

 ## MATH MEMORIES

"No one in my family is good at math. I guess we just don't have math genes. I just assumed that I would never succeed at understanding it, so I avoided math whenever I could."

"The math part of my brain has atrophied. It would be easier for me to learn Greek. I can't even understand the basic principles."

"I need to acquire a basic understanding of math without a teacher yelling and screaming at me, because I am slow to grasp difficult concepts."

"When I take a math test, I usually go blank. Time goes by very quickly, and I know I need more time than I have to finish it."

"I really hate math tests. I break out into a sweat, my head hurts, and I start to panic."

*"I had a difficult time in high school because I began to question **why** you did things a certain way. The teachers never gave me an answer I completely understood, so I became impatient and more uncomfortable with math."*

CHOOSING THE RIGHT MATH COURSE

Signing up to take a mathematics course is often the first step most people take to conquer their math anxiety. The class you end up taking and when you take it may mean the difference between becoming a successful mathematics student and prolonging your misery.

Most schools offer a placement test to determine the course that is appropriate for your skill level. If you are placed in a "low-level" course, such as arithmetic or prealgebra, that does not carry academic credit, you may be tempted to skip to the next course. This is not a wise idea, unless you are willing to learn enough mathematics on your own to master all the material in the course you want to skip. It is always important for you to be thoroughly competent and confident in your ability to do all the prerequisite work before you begin any math course. Otherwise, you begin the course with a serious handicap, and you may not have ample time to catch up before the course is over. If you think that a math course may be especially difficult, consider auditing the course before you take it for credit to brush up on your skills.

Math is a cumulative body of knowledge, and learning it is similar to learning a foreign language. Most of us would not think of enrolling in an advanced course in Spanish or Japanese unless we were confident in our ability to speak and read the language at the level that was required for that course. Mathematics courses should be regarded in the same way. If you did not do well on a placement test because you forgot the math you once knew, you must still relearn that material to be successful in the next course. Just because a mathematical concept seems familiar to you does not mean that you are skilled at applying it.

If you have a choice in instructors for a math course, talk to other students who have taken classes with the various instructors, and if possible, sit in on one of their classes. Professors who give little homework and easy tests may not be the best choice for preparing you to do well in a more advanced course. Try to find an instructor whose teaching style is clear and well-organized and who is available after class for extra help if you need it. Different students find it easier to learn from instructors with different teaching styles. If you can, you may want to sit in on more than one class to find the instructor who is best suited to your needs.

It may be beneficial to choose a math class that meets at least two or three times a week, rather than a class that meets only once a week. A class that meets more frequently will help motivate you to study the material on a regular basis, since you will probably be required to complete assignments prior to every class. You will also have more opportunities each week to ask questions about the homework or get clarification on concepts that you do not fully understand.

Make sure that you have enough time in your schedule every week to do all the work required in a math course. Math courses can be extremely time-consuming and may require twice as much time as another subject that carries the same number of credits. You may have to organize your time carefully so that you can balance your time between mathematics and other courses, in addition to any extracurricular activities, work, or family responsibilities you may have. Keep in mind that it is better to take fewer courses and do well in all of them than to take too many and run the risk of doing poorly. It is usually better to plan your courses so that you take math in successive semesters. This will help ensure that you do not forget the prerequisite material for each class. However, if a semester is exceptionally busy, you may have to delay taking a math course until your schedule improves. If you are unable to spend the time you need to thoroughly learn the material covered in a mathematics course, you are increasing your chances of failure.

GETTING THE MOST OUT OF A MATH CLASS

When you are taking a math course, it is extremely important to attend every class. To understand the material presented in each class, you must have mastered the topics presented in previous classes. Missing just one class could make it difficult for you to learn whatever else is presented in the rest of the course. If you don't catch up, that could mean the difference between success and failure. If you do need to miss a class, arrange to get a copy of the notes from a reliable classmate, try to complete the homework, and if necessary, see the instructor for additional help. You should also find out if your school has a videotape available for you to view that covers the material you have missed. Make sure you schedule time to watch the video and take notes before the next class. If you know in advance that you will miss a class, get the assignment ahead of time, and try to complete it so that you will not be behind the rest of the class when you return.

Before each class, do all the assigned homework, and come prepared to ask questions about any problems you had difficulty solving. If part of the class is spent reviewing homework problems, make a list of the problems you would like the teacher to work out, and have it available when the class begins. Many students waste time in class shuffling through papers and never get their questions answered. If you have time, it is helpful to read the material in your textbook that will be covered in the next class. This will give you some familiarity with the subject and make it easier for you to understand what will be presented in the next lecture.

When you come to class, sit where you can hear the instructor and see everything on the board, so that you will be able to take good notes. Often students having trouble with math sit in the back of the room, to avoid being asked a question. Students in the back of the room are often less involved in class discussions and may find it more difficult to pay attention, which compounds their difficulties. Some students tape-record classes. I do not recommend this, because it takes a lot of time after class to listen to a tape and to transcribe it. Instead, make the most of your time by developing the listening skills needed to create a well-organized and complete set of notes during class.

Effective note-taking is perhaps one of the most valuable skills you can acquire to ensure your success. It is also one of the most difficult to master since it involves coordinating the activities of seeing, listening, writing, and understanding, all within a time period set by the pace of the instructor. It is important that you bring all the tools you will need to fully participate in the class. This includes an extra pen or pencil, an eraser, highlighters or colored pencils to emphasize important material, copies of homework assignments or tests, and your textbook. Some students prefer to take notes in pen; others prefer pencil, so that they can easily erase mistakes. Be certain to record the date on all handouts, homework assignments, and notes. In addition to a bound notebook, you may want to get a multipocket folder for all other course materials. As the instructor presents the material, write down as much as you can, while paying attention to what is being said. Make sure that your notes are neat, clear, and complete. Include every step of every problem in addition to the explanations provided. When the instructor refers to a problem or other material from the textbook, write down the page number so you can refer to it later. You may also want to highlight areas of the text that are discussed during class. If you don't understand something written on the board or said by the instructor, write it down anyway and highlight that point in your notes, to help you remember to get clarification. While it is preferable to understand all your notes as you write them down, it is better to continue to record everything presented in the class than to stop taking notes so that you can figure out what was discussed a few minutes ago.

When the instructor says something during class that you don't understand, ask a question. Often, many students in the class have the same question. It is foolish to avoid asking a question because you think others may view it as a "dumb question." Since getting your questions answered will illuminate your understanding of a topic, no question can be considered dumb. While it is important to get answers to *your* questions, do not become distracted by questions from other students. If you understand what the instructor is explaining, but another student's question confuses you, it may be best to ignore it. If too many questions are asked during a class, the instructor may have to move on to the next topic without further explanation. If the class moves ahead and you still do not understand something, make note of where you got lost and get help from the instructor after class or during the instructor's office hours.

After each class ends, review your notes as soon as you can, to reinforce your understanding of the material you have learned. Add further explanations to your notes to ensure that you understand topics you may have found confusing. If you find that you are frequently lost in class, or that your notes don't make sense, you may have to put more time into familiarizing yourself with the upcoming topics before attending the next class.

Here is a summary of what you can do to get the most out of a math class.

Building Classroom Competence

1. Attend every class.
2. Come prepared with completed assignments and questions on topics you do not understand.
3. Sit where you can see and hear everything being presented.
4. Bring assignments, notes, books, and all other materials you will need to class.
5. Date all notes, handouts, assignments, and tests.
6. Make certain that your notes are neat, clear, and complete.
7. Continue taking notes, even if you get lost, and highlight areas where you need help.
8. If you don't understand something, ask a question.
9. Review your notes shortly after the class ends to reinforce your understanding.

YOUR ATTITUDE TOWARD MATHEMATICS

While you are attending a math class, doing your math homework, or taking a math test, it is important that you pay attention to the dialogue that is going on in your mind. Negative thoughts do not help you to solve a problem; they only serve to fuel your math anxiety. If you find yourself getting confused in the middle of a mathematics lecture, don't panic. Ask a question; or if you are unable to do so, mark the place in your notebook where you got lost, so that you can get help after class. Don't worry if you do not understand everything the instructor is saying; just continue to take notes. Often, you will find that you are able to understand more by working out problems on your own, while referring to your class notes or the textbook.

As you work on a math problem, talk yourself through it. Mathematical notation is very precise and concise. A few symbols can represent many complex ideas. If you try to mentally translate the symbols into words, you will begin to understand the relationships between mathematical notation and the techniques used to solve a problem. This will also help you take a stepwise approach to solving problems. Many times, to solve a problem, you need to break it down into a series of smaller steps, working on one step at a time before moving on to the next one. Talking yourself through a problem will help you clarify your thinking process so that you can organize a problem-solving strategy into a series of steps.

Always do enough problems so that you feel confident with each newly acquired skill. This may mean doing more problems than are assigned in the homework. Begin with the simplest problems, and then move on to more complicated ones. If you forget how to solve a problem, think of a simple example to remind you of the technique. Use your textbook and class notes to look up techniques you may have forgotten or never understood clearly. If you find that you are always forgetting the same techniques, it probably means that you have not done enough practice problems to thoroughly learn the methods needed to solve them.

Students sometimes have access to solutions manuals that accompany their textbooks. Although looking at worked-out solutions can help you figure out how to solve difficult problems, it is easy to become dependent on a solutions manual rather than spend the time needed to solve problems on your own. Therefore, be sure that you acquire the skills needed to solve a variety of problems at varying levels of difficulty without looking up the solution.

It is also extremely important that you cultivate a positive attitude toward your mistakes. Everyone makes lots of mistakes in doing math. One of the main ways we learn how to do something correctly is to learn what does *not* work. Many times, a certain strategy for solving a problem will not work, and you will have to start again from the beginning. Don't let that discourage you. A series of "false starts" often lets you eliminate possibilities that don't work, leading you to the correct solution to the problem. In fact, sometimes you gain a more thorough understanding of a problem, and you can better remember what you did when you arrive at a solution by trial and error.

Build confidence in your ability by noting your successes. Allow yourself to take pride in your accomplishments, and don't scold yourself for your failures. However, be wary of overconfidence that may cause you to stop studying before you have completely mastered the material to be learned.

STRATEGIES FOR EFFECTIVE STUDYING

While you are taking a math class, it is very important that you study regularly. Even if homework is not collected, finish each assignment before every class, so that you are prepared to ask questions and get the most out of class. If you come to class unprepared, you will not benefit as much from questions regarding the homework, because the problems will be unfamiliar to you. Also, you may become confused when the instructor presents new material, because you will not yet have mastered the concepts that form its foundation. It is also essential that you practice doing math on a regular basis, even when the class is over, to prevent yourself from forgetting what you have learned and losing the skills you have acquired.

It is best to schedule a set period of time to study math every day, or at least every other day. For some people, this may be the first thing in the morning, when their minds are the clearest. For others, it may be immediately after math class when the material is still fresh in mind. Your study time should be organized so that you have no distractions and can work without interruptions. Schedule short breaks during your sessions to prevent drowsiness and allow yourself an opportunity to assimilate what you have learned. It is much more productive to study math for an hour a day than to attempt to cram all your studying into a seven-hour-long marathon session once a week.

The total study time you will need to be successful depends on a number of factors, such as how well prepared you are for the course, how quickly you are able to learn new material, and how productive you can be during the time you allocate for homework. You may find that you need to spend at least twice as much time studying math as you do studying any other subject. Do not waste an entire study session on one problem. If you are not making progress because you are frustrated, distracted, or tired, take a break and come back to it later. Manage your time wisely. You need to strike the right balance between a sense of discipline that makes your study time productive, and a sense of relaxation that enables you to maintain a high level of concentration. Be realistic about how much time you need to thoroughly master the material and how much time you actually have, given other priorities in your life.

When you are doing math homework, I strongly recommend that you work in pencil. Put a large eraser at the end of your pencil, and expect to use it frequently. Show all your work neatly and clearly, even if you do not have to hand in the assignment. This will help you develop good work habits for taking tests, and it will make it easier for you to find mistakes. Work slowly and check your work after every step, to avoid careless mistakes. Resist the temptation to scribble intermediate calculations in margins or on "scrap" paper, because this will make it difficult for you to go back through the problem to check your work.

Use the answers in the back of the book appropriately. Just because you can look up the answer to see if you did the problem correctly, do not rush through a problem without checking your work. This is a bad habit that will prevent you from doing well on tests, because you will not have developed the skill for finding mistakes on your own.

If you find that you cannot do any of the homework problems, do a problem that is worked out in your textbook, or work out a problem that was done in class, while referring to your notes. Then cover up the solution, and try to do the same problem on your own. It may take a bit of time and patience, but the more problems you do, the more the procedures for solving them will stick in your mind.

If you find the first few problems in a homework assignment to be very easy, do not be misled into thinking that you do not have to finish the assignment. In most textbooks, the problems are arranged in order of difficulty, with the easiest ones appearing first. You will probably be tested on problems of varying levels of difficulty, not just the easiest ones. In some cases, even though you have done all the assigned homework, you still may not feel confident in your ability to work out all the problems on your own. It is then your responsibility to do additional problems until you feel that you have thoroughly mastered each mathematical technique. Many textbooks also present problems in "pairs" so that problems 1 and 2 are at similar levels of difficulty. Therefore, if you need extra practice at a certain level of difficulty, try the other problem in the pair, even if it was not assigned.

Learning math does not require a lot of memorization. Instead, it is important that you practice solving lots of problems with an understanding of the mathematical techniques needed to solve them. This will help you remember the method that should be applied to each type of problem and the steps that must be followed to arrive at a solution. However, some important facts must be memorized, such as multiplication tables, geometric formulas, and conversion factors for equivalent units of measurement. To help you memorize these, you may want to put up signs around your home, or make flash cards for yourself.

Choose study techniques that bring you success. To learn the material, some students rely more on class notes, and others rely more on the textbook. Some students join study groups or meet regularly with a tutor, while others prefer to work on their own. Many people prefer short study sessions with lots of breaks, and others accomplish more when they focus on a subject for a longer period of uninterrupted time. Techniques that work well for one student may not be much help to another.

Here is a summary of some of the strategies you can use to study math effectively:

Study Strategies

1. As soon as the class begins, establish a regular schedule to study math frequently.

2. Plan short breaks during your study sessions to prevent drowsiness and keep motivated.

3. Don't cram for exams or force yourself to study when exhausted, frustrated, or distracted.

4. Manage your study time wisely, striking the right balance between discipline and relaxation.

5. Show all your work neatly and clearly, to develop good test-taking habits.

6. Develop skills for finding mistakes without relying on looking up the answers.

7. Do as many problems as you need to do, to thoroughly master each technique.

8. Use flash cards or other devices to memorize required facts and formulas.

9. Choose study techniques that bring you success.

ESTIMATION

Estimation is critical to catching "obvious" errors and making sure that the answers are reasonable. Throughout this book, I give examples of how to come up with a quick approximation for the right answer, before actually working through a problem. Anytime you use a pocket calculator, you should have an estimated answer in mind before pressing the "=" button. In using calculators, many careless mistakes occur from pushing the wrong button, and these can easily be spotted if the answer in the calculator window is not close to the estimate. Developing good approximation skills will also give you greater confidence in your answers, even when you are not using a calculator. Often, students reject an answer because it does not "look right," only to find out later that it was correct. For example, you may think that if two test problems in a row have the same answer, one must be wrong. If you are able to see that an answer you obtained is reasonable by comparing it to your estimate, you will be less likely to change it.

HOW TO "READ" A MATH BOOK

To use a math book effectively, you cannot simply "read" it in the same way you would read a novel or a history book. There are a variety of strategies you can use, and the ones you choose may vary from section to section, depending upon how well you understand the material being presented. For example, if you did not have any difficulty with the material presented in class, you might first try working out a few homework problems and only refer to the examples in the text if you had trouble solving them. But if you were confused by an instructor's lecture, you might first try to read the section of the text that precedes the homework problems.

As you read the material, have a pencil and paper available so that you can work out the problems as you read through them. A good text will often have explanations next to each step of the solutions to help you understand what techniques were used and why they were chosen. Highlight important information and write notes in the margins, so that key points stand out when you are reviewing for a test.

Do not skip over terms you do not understand. Many words used in mathematics have very precise meanings, and a vague recollection of a word will not be enough for you to follow a discussion. If you have forgotten the meaning of a word, look in the index to find out where in the text it was previously explained. Keep your old math books from prerequisite courses. They will be invaluable references as you proceed to more difficult courses. You can use these books to look up the meanings of mathematical terms and to refresh the problem-solving techniques that you have forgotten.

USING ADDITIONAL RESOURCES

Take advantage of your instructor's office hours to obtain extra help outside of class. Come well prepared with questions regarding the lecture and homework problems you had difficulty completing. Some of my students have been able to accomplish more during a 15-minute session than others accomplish in an hour, because they organized all their questions ahead of time. Other students waste a lot of time in my office looking through their notes for questions and paging through the text to find difficult problems. It is particularly important to prepare a list of questions before coming for help, especially if your instructor generally sees a lot of students during office hours.

Many schools provide extra help for math students through tutoring services and math labs. Before you meet with a tutor, prepare a list a questions so that you can make the most of your time. Also, be aware that some free tutors are required to limit the time they can spend with any one student. If there are many tutors available, try to find one whom you are comfortable working with, and who can explain the material to you in a way that you understand. Spending time with a tutor is not a substitute for studying on your own; so make sure to allow time in your schedule for both tutoring and independent study. Math labs often have computer programs that supplement the textbook, so you can get additional practice working out certain types of problems. Be careful not to waste a lot of time checking out all the available software if it is not proving effective in helping you master the material covered in your math class.

Depending on your schedule, it may be helpful to study with other students in the class. Helping another student understand how to solve a problem will solidify your own understanding of the material. However, do not rely on a study group as a substitute for individual studying, and be wary of groups that spend most of the time socializing instead of studying.

If you find that the math book assigned for your class is confusing, ask the instructor to recommend another book you could purchase to supplement it. Often, seeing the same type of problem that appears in the assigned text explained in a different way will clear up your confusion. Many excellent review books and outline series are available in the reference section of most bookstores. Examine a book carefully before you buy it, to determine whether it will be helpful to you. Sometimes, one book will make more sense to you on one topic, and another book will make more sense to you on another topic.

Always keep your old math books. Over time, they will provide you with an important reference library that you can use to look up unfamiliar terms and to review mathematical techniques you may have forgotten.

TEST PREPARATION

It is never too early to begin studying for a math test. In fact, you should begin studying for the first test on the first day of class, and you should begin studying for the second test immediately after taking the first test. Cramming the night before a math test is an open invitation to panic on the day of the test. The skills you need to master to be successful in mathematics cannot be learned overnight and need to be acquired over a period of time.

The most effective strategy for being a successful mathematics student is to schedule plenty of time throughout the semester to study math. Do the assigned homework before every class, to be certain that you do not fall behind. Review what you have already studied a few times a week, to ensure that you have not forgotten concepts that will be crucial to your understanding of new material. The key to success is to *practice, practice, practice*. You need to work out lots of problems before you become proficient in applying a mathematical technique, even if you seem to "get it" after working out only one problem. If you apply this strategy, by the time the week before a test arrives, you will have already completed a major portion of your studying.

When you review for a test, study all the material thoroughly. Do not skip a topic just because you think that it won't be on the test. Your goal should be to get every problem on the test correct, not merely to pass. If you avoid becoming proficient in certain techniques because they are difficult, or if you are not completely confident in the material you have studied, you run the risk of having a "mental block" while you are taking the test.

A *mental block* is a sudden interruption in a thought process. It is caused by a sense of panic that overcomes students when they are unable to solve a problem on a test. They sometimes become so overwhelmed that they have difficulty not only with the first problem they could not solve, but also with the rest of the test. Mental blocks usually occur when students have not adequately prepared for the test and lose confidence in their ability to complete it successfully. They often lose their ability to concentrate and are even unable to complete the problems they had no difficulty with before the test. The best way to avoid a mental block is to be thoroughly prepared to answer any type of problem that could be asked on a test. This allows you to remain completely confident in your ability to do well throughout the duration of the test.

If your instructor is giving an *open-book test*, find out what materials you will be allowed to bring. Even if you are allowed to bring your textbook and your notes, take time to make a list of the techniques and formulas you are most likely to need. You can waste a lot of valuable time during open-book tests by paging through books and notes to find out how to solve a problem. Regardless of whether a test is closed- or open-book, it is critical that you thoroughly study all the material that is going to be tested, so that you increase your likelihood of success.

Before a test, it is a good idea to make up a "practice test" for yourself that includes a representative sample of all the different types of problems that are likely to be asked. Your textbook is a good source of problems, especially if it has a section of review problems or a chapter test at the end of every chapter. Make a note of where each problem came from so that you can check your answers later. Mix up the problems so that they are not in any particular order with regard to subject matter or level or difficulty. Then set aside a period of time to complete the practice test; allow the same time that will be allowed for the actual test. Simulate actual test conditions. Work in a place with no distractions, and do not refer to your notes or to the textbook if you have difficulty solving a problem. Use as much of the allotted time as you need to complete the test, and then check your work. When you are finished, or when your time is up, look up the answers and grade the test. This exercise will help you to determine on which types of problems you need to spend additional time studying.

When you get a test back, try to determine how your instructor chose the problems and how partial credit was assigned to problems you solved incorrectly. If you do badly on a test, resist the temptation to throw it out. Instead, look it over carefully to determine where you made mistakes, and work through each problem as many times as you need to solve it correctly. At the end of the semester, use your old tests as guides for making up a practice final exam.

TEST-TAKING STRATEGIES

Before any test, be certain to get a good night's sleep. Staying up all night to study usually does not help you learn math; it just makes you feel exhausted the next day. If you have not gotten enough sleep, you may find it difficult to concentrate during a test, and you will not do your best.

On the day of a math test, arrive early and pick a comfortable seat, so that you will not be in a state of panic when the test begins. Make sure that you have at least two sharpened pencils, a big eraser, and a watch to keep track of the time. When you first receive the test, look it over completely before you begin, and estimate how much time you should spend on each problem so that you can pace yourself appropriately.

Work slowly and carefully, and check your work after every step. Do not race through the test, thinking that you will have enough time to work out every problem twice, because if you run out of time, you may be forced to turn in a test filled with a lot of careless mistakes. If you get stuck on a problem, don't panic, but proceed to the next one. You can go back to it later, after completing the rest of the test.

Show all work and attempt to solve every problem. If you do not get the correct answer, you may be eligible for partial credit. If time permits, check and recheck all your work. There is no point in handing in your test before the time is up, if you could have used the time to find and correct some mistakes, resulting in a higher score.

Sometimes, in spite of all our preparations, we start to panic while we are taking a math test. One technique you can use to calm your anxiety is to stop for a moment and simply notice your thoughts. You may find that you are thinking that you should have studied more, or that the test is more difficult than you expected, or that you wish you were somewhere else. Remind yourself that continuing with this negative thought pattern will not help you finish the test and will only increase your anxiety. Then take a few deep breaths and start over, trying your best to concentrate on solving the problem at hand. This approach can also help us to get back on track when we find ourselves daydreaming. Its purpose is to interrupt the cascade of distracting thoughts, which can go on for long periods of time if we are not aware of what is happening.

It is best to first try this technique while you are preparing for a math test, so that you have some actual experience of it helping you to resume your concentration. At first, it may be difficult or even frightening for you to stop and pay attention to what you are thinking when you feel anxious. If you notice that you are daydreaming, you may find that you want to continue to let your thoughts wander, instead of bringing your focus back to solving math problems. However, the more you practice this technique and benefit from using it, the more likely you are to remember to apply it in test situations.

Here is a summary of some of the things you can do to perform better on tests:

Test-Taking Tips

1. Begin studying early so that you are thoroughly prepared in advance.

2. Avoid mental blocks by learning all the material well enough to feel confident.

3. Make up a practice test that includes all types of problems you might be asked to do.

4. Get a good night's sleep on the night before a test.

5. Arrive early for the test and pick a comfortable seat.

6. Bring at least two sharpened pencils, an eraser, and a watch to keep track of time.

7. Look over the test before you begin, and estimate the time you can spend on each problem.

8. Work slowly and carefully, and check your work after every step.

9. If you get stuck on a problem, don't panic, but go on to the next one.

10. Show all your work and attempt to solve every problem.

11. If you finish early, check and recheck every problem to catch mistakes.

12. To calm anxiety, stop, notice your thoughts, take deep breaths, and start over.

HOW TO MEASURE RESULTS

After you get back a math test, it is important to look at not only your grade, but also the types of problems you had difficulty solving correctly. If you could not solve many different types of problems, you may need to review the material much more thoroughly than if you had trouble with only one type of problem. If you thought that you knew the material much better than your grade reflects, check for careless mistakes. To improve your performance on the next test, you may just have to concentrate on working more carefully and checking your work more frequently.

If you pass a test with a grade of C or lower, you need to put much greater effort into studying the material covered by that test, in addition to studying the new material for the next test, which creates additional demands on your time. The sooner you begin to do well, the better prepared you will be for the final exam.

It is not good enough to barely pass a math course. The lower your final grade, the more likely it is that you will have trouble in the next math course, or in other courses that require the use of mathematics. You will eventually need to learn all the material covered in a math course, so you might as well learn it while you are taking the course and get an A. If you take a math course with a "lenient instructor," your grade may not reflect how well you know the material. Only you can accurately assess how prepared you are for the next course.

Even if you pass a math course with a high grade, the next course may be difficult for you if you wait too long to take it. Being away from math for one semester, or during a summer vacation, may cause you to forget important concepts. If this is the case, before you proceed to the next course, plan time in your schedule to review material you may have forgotten.

As mentioned earlier, learning mathematics is very much like learning a foreign language or learning to play a musical instrument. Mathematics is a cumulative body of knowledge, and a failure to master one concept may prevent you from understanding something else later on. A lot of practice is required to become proficient in mathematics. When a musician performs, it is obvious if he has not rehearsed enough, even if he is familiar with the piece. When someone speaks a foreign language, even if she knows the vocabulary, it is easy to detect whether she is fluent in that language. Mathematics is very similar in this way. Simply having a superficial understanding of the material is not enough to do well. To do well on a math test, you must develop your skills to the level that enables you to complete all the problems accurately in the time allotted. To be successful in mathematics, always aim for the highest standard, and apply the time and energy necessary to achieve this goal.

STRATEGIES FOR SUCCESS

Here is a summary of the strategies we have discussed in this chapter to help you conquer math anxiety:

STRATEGIES FOR SUCCESS IN CONQUERING MATH ANXIETY

1. Master the prerequisites before you take a math course.

2. Attend every class, come prepared with questions, and take thorough notes.

3. Don't fuel negative thoughts, and cultivate a positive attitude toward your mistakes.

4. Set aside a regular time to study math, and do all the homework before every class.

5. Estimate answers so that you can catch obvious mistakes, especially when you are using a calculator.

6. Work out problems as you read a math book, and look up unfamiliar terms.

7. Come prepared with specific questions when you seek extra help.

8. Begin studying for tests early to prevent mental blocks.

9. Work slowly and carefully when you take a test, and check your work after every step.

10. Aim for a high grade so that you are prepared for the next math course.

CHAPTER 2 EXERCISES

1. Make a log to keep track of the time you spend studying math. Did you study math regularly, or were there long gaps between sessions? When are your most favorite and least favorite times of day to study? Are you more productive during longer or shorter study sessions?

2. Where do you prefer to sit during a math class—in the front or back of the room or somewhere in the middle? Try sitting in another location during your next class. Did you notice anything different about your experience when you sat elsewhere?

3. What do you do when you find that your mind is distracted while you are trying to study math? Do you take a break and do something else? What activities do you find to be most beneficial in helping you to maintain your concentration?

4. The next time you have difficulty working out a math homework problem, stop for a moment and write down some of the thoughts that are going through your mind. Were these thoughts creating anxiety? Were you daydreaming? Take a few deep breaths and try again to solve the problem. What helped you to complete the problem successfully?

5. What steps did you take to prepare for your last math test? What particular things did you do that helped you achieve a higher grade?

6. Try using two additional strategies discussed in this chapter to help you become a better math student. Describe whether or not you found them to be useful.

3

Becoming Nimble with Numbers

 ## MATH MEMORIES

"Today my job requires me to do addition and subtraction very quickly, and I am very frustrated and embarrassed by not being able to do simple arithmetic, while everyone else can."

"My big problem in grammar school was those awful multiplication tables. My mother would help me memorize flash cards at home, and when I got to school I would forget everything. When we got to division, I could not solve the problems because I could not remember the multiplication facts."

"Memorizing multiplication tables kept me up many nights, anxious and sweating. I didn't learn them until 5th grade. By junior high school, I hated math so much that I avoided it, except when I crammed for a test. Since I never grasped the basics, it never made sense to me, so I stopped taking math as soon as I could."

"Our 2nd grade teacher would drill us in multiplication tables by tossing a bean bag at us while giving us two numbers to multiply. When we caught the bag, we were supposed to say the answer. That really put us on the spot! Ever since then I have been very anxious about math."

 ## COMMON PROBLEMS

Even though we see numbers constantly in daily life, we are often baffled by situations that require us to perform even the simplest calculations. A major reason for this difficulty is that we have forgotten the techniques for doing basic calculations such as addition, subtraction, multiplication, and division. While most of us do not hesitate to pick up a dictionary when we have forgotten how to spell a word, when we forget how to multiply two numbers, we are not in the habit of looking up the procedure in a math book. In fact, many of us did not even own a math book until we needed to purchase one for a math course.

When we try to read a math book, the terminology used to describe various mathematical procedures often makes it difficult for us to figure out what to do. Multiplication can be particularly difficult if we do not remember the multiplication tables. Division is probably one of the most difficult operations to perform because it requires so many steps and problems take a long time to solve.

Finally, word problems are a major source of anxiety for most people because we feel that if we do not *immediately* know how to solve the problem, we will never arrive at a solution.

HINTS FOR STUDYING NUMBERS

The first step toward gaining confidence in working with numbers is to thoroughly learn the procedures for adding, subtracting, multiplying, and dividing the numbers we use most frequently, which are the whole numbers. **Whole numbers** include 0, 1, 2, 3, 4, 5, 6, 7, 8, 9, 10, 11, 12, 13, 14, 15, · · · . The three dots indicate that there is no end to the list of whole numbers. In mathematics, we express this by saying that there are an **infinite** number of whole numbers.

The 10 numerals 0 to 9 are sometimes called **digits,** because the 10 fingers were originally used for counting. The word *digit* means finger or toe.

Numbers are named according to the location or **place value** of each digit. For example, the number 7,423,681 is read as "seven million, four hundred twenty-three thousand, six hundred eighty-one." Each group of three digits, separated by a comma, is called a **period.** The place value of each digit is shown in Figure 3.1.

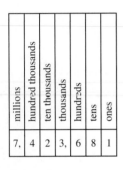

millions	hundred thousands	ten thousands	thousands	hundreds	tens	ones
7,	4	2	3,	6	8	1

Figure 3.1

It is also very important that you understand the terminology used to describe ideas and procedures in mathematics. Math books cannot be read as quickly as a novel, or even a history book. Whenever you encounter a word you do not understand, look it up in the index to find a clearer explanation of its meaning. If you ever forget how to solve a problem, first think of a simpler problem that you can solve by using the same technique, to help remind you what to do. Then if you need to, look up the procedure for solving that type of problem in a math book.

Even though being successful in math does not require a lot of memorization, it is critical that you memorize the multiplication tables. Otherwise, it will take you much longer to solve even the simplest problems, and you will lose track of what to do next when solving more complicated problems. It is also helpful to become familiar with the multistep process for dividing whole numbers. When you are doing long division or performing any lengthy mathematical calculation, it is extremely important to work slowly and carefully and to check your work after every step to avoid careless mistakes.

To overcome anxiety in dealing with word problems, use a stepwise approach in working through the problem. Don't worry if the solution is not immediately apparent to you, but do try to come up with a plan of action, and focus on one step at a time. We will discuss word problems in greater detail at the end of this chapter.

SYMBOLS USED IN MATHEMATICS

Mathematics may seem intimidating to us if we do not understand the short-hand notation that is used to convey mathematical concepts. When you study music, you need to learn not only how to play an instrument but also how to read a musical score. Otherwise, you would not know which notes to play, how loud to play them, or how to time the melody. Likewise, when you are studying mathematics, it is important not only to learn how to do various techniques, but also to understand the meaning of the mathematical notation that tells you which operations to perform. This table summarizes the common mathematical symbols used to compare numbers and represent the basic operations:

Symbols Used in Mathematics

Name	*Symbol*	*Example*	*Meaning*
Equality	$=$	$8 = 8$	8 is equal to 8
Inequality	$\neq$	$72 \neq 27$	72 is not equal to 27
Approximate equality	$\approx$	$497 \approx 500$	497 is approximately equal to 500
Greater than	$>$	$6 > 3$	6 is greater than 3
Less than	$<$	$29 < 92$	29 is less than 92
Addition	$+$	$5 + 8$	Add 5 and 8
Subtraction	$-$	$11 - 6$	Subtract 6 from 11
Multiplication	$\times$	2×5	Multiply 2 and 5
Division	$\div$	$12 \div 3$	Divide 12 by 3

ADDITION OF WHOLE NUMBERS

Addition is one of the simplest operations to perform, once you know the technique. We will begin by defining some words associated with addition. The numbers to be added are called **addends.** The answer is called the **sum.** The word *sum* is more commonly used than the word *addends*. An addition problem may be written horizontally or vertically as shown here.

$$7 \quad + \quad 9 \quad = \quad 16 \qquad\qquad 7 \quad \text{addend}$$
$$\uparrow \qquad\quad \uparrow \qquad\quad \uparrow \qquad\qquad \underline{+\ 9} \quad \text{addend}$$
$$\text{addend} \quad \text{addend} \quad \text{sum} \qquad 16 \quad \text{sum}$$

It is usually easiest to solve an addition problem by using a vertical format.

ADDITION IN DAILY LIFE: TOTAL MILEAGE

Consider the following example. A computer sales representative drove 278 miles from Detroit to Indianapolis on Monday and 235 miles from Indianapolis to St. Louis on Tuesday. What is the total number of miles the sales representative drove in those 2 days? To solve this problem, we add $278 + 235$.

First we will estimate the answer by adding approximate values. The symbol $\approx$ means "approximately equal to."

$$278 \approx \quad 300 \qquad \text{Since 278 is closer to 300 than to 200}$$
$$\underline{+\ 235} \approx \underline{+\ 200} \qquad \text{Since 235 is closer to 200 than to 300}$$
$$500 \qquad \text{Add } 200 + 300 = 500$$

The estimated answer is 500 miles. It is very important to first estimate answers whenever you can, especially when you are using a calculator. This simple technique does not take a lot of time and can help you catch many careless mistakes.

Let us now determine the exact answer. To add whole numbers, we write the numbers vertically, lining up digits having the same place value. We then add the digits in each column, moving from right to left. If the sum of the digits in any column is greater than 9, we carry the value of the number in the tens place to the next column. This procedure is called **carrying.**

$$\overset{1\ 1}{278} \qquad 8 + 5 = 13. \text{ Write down 3. Carry 1 to the tens place.}$$
$$\underline{+\ 235} \qquad 1 + 7 + 3 = 11. \text{ Write down 1. Carry 1 to the hundreds place.}$$
$$513 \qquad 1 + 2 + 2 = 5. \text{ Write down 5.}$$

Therefore, the sales representative drove 513 miles in 2 days. Since this is close to our estimate of 500 miles, this answer is reasonable. Here is a summary of the procedure to add whole numbers.

To Add Whole Numbers

1. Write the numbers to be added in a column, lining up digits having the same place value.
2. Add the digits in each column while moving from right to left.
3. If the sum of the digits in any column exceeds 9, write down the digit in the ones place and carry the digit in the tens place to the next column.

SUBTRACTION OF WHOLE NUMBERS

Subtraction of whole numbers is a bit more complicated than addition. However, once we have mastered this technique, our biggest obstacle to success will be working too quickly, resulting in careless mistakes. Subtraction is actually the reverse of addition. For example,

$$\text{if} \quad 8 + 5 = 13 \quad \text{then} \quad 13 - 5 = 8$$

In a subtraction problem, the first number is called the **minuend,** the second number is called the **subtrahend,** and the answer is called the **difference.** The word *difference* is more commonly used than the words *minuend* and *subtrahend.* As with addition, a subtraction problem can be written horizontally or vertically, as shown here.

$$15 \quad - \quad 9 \quad = \quad 6 \qquad\qquad 15 \quad \text{minuend}$$

$$\uparrow \qquad\qquad \uparrow \qquad\qquad \uparrow \qquad\qquad \underline{-\ 9} \quad \text{subtrahend}$$

minuend   subtrahend   difference   6   difference

To check the answer to a subtraction problem, we can add the difference to the subtrahend. The result should equal the minuend.

Check: 6   difference

$$\underline{+\ 9} \qquad \text{subtrahend}$$

15   √   minuend

We can often perform the check to a subtraction problem mentally.

SUBTRACTION IN DAILY LIFE: POPULATION EXPANSION

Let us now look at an example of a problem using the operation subtraction. If the population of a small town in Vermont is now 6,032 and last year the population was 5,817, by how much did the population increase? To solve this problem, we subtract 6,032 − 5,817. We will first estimate the answer.

$$6,032 \approx \quad 6,000 \qquad \text{Since 6,032 is closer to 6,000 than to 6,100}$$

$$\underline{-\ 5,817} \approx \underline{-\ 5,800} \qquad \text{Since 5,817 is closer to 5,800 than to 5,900}$$

$$200 \qquad 6,000 - 5,800 = 200$$

The estimated answer is 200 people. To determine the exact answer, we write the problem vertically, lining up digits with the same place value. We then subtract the digits in each column, moving from right to left. If the digit on top is smaller than the digit below it in the same column, we borrow 1 from the digit to its left and add 10 to that digit. This process is called **borrowing.**

$$
\begin{array}{r}
6,0\ 3\ 2 \\
-\ 5,8\ 1\ 7 \\
\hline
\end{array}
\qquad
\begin{array}{r}
{}^{5}\quad {}^{2} \\
\cancel{6},{}^{1}0\,\cancel{3}{}^{1}2 \\
-\ 5,8\ 1\ 7 \\
\hline
2\ 1\ 5
\end{array}
$$

Since 2 < 7, borrow 1 from 3 in the tens column and add 10 to 2 in the ones column, to get 12 ones. 12 − 7 = 5.   2 − 1 = 1.

Since 0 < 8, borrow 1 from 6 in the thousands column and add 10 to 0 in the hundreds column, to get 10 hundreds. 10 − 8 = 2.   5 − 5 = 0.

Therefore, the population increased by 215 people. Since this is close to our estimate of 200, this answer is reasonable. To check our answer, we add 215 to 5,817 and make sure that the result equals 6,032.

$$
\begin{array}{r}
{\scriptstyle 1 \quad 1} \\
\text{Check:} \qquad 215 \\
+\ 5{,}817 \\
\hline
6{,}032 \quad \surd \qquad \text{The answer checks.}
\end{array}
$$

SUBTRACTION IN DAILY LIFE: BANK DEPOSIT

When the top number contains lots of zeros, you may need to do lots of borrowing, as shown in the next example. Suppose that you earned a $10,000 bonus and decided to use it to purchase a laptop computer and then to deposit the rest into a bank account. If the laptop costs $1,049, how much will you have left to deposit into the bank? Let's first estimate the answer. Since $1,049 \approx \$1,000$ and $\$10,000 - \$1,000 = \$9,000$, the answer should be close to $9,000. Now let's determine the exact answer.

$$
\begin{array}{r}
{\scriptstyle 0\ \ 9\ \ 9\ \ 9} \\
10{,}0\,0\,0 \qquad \ \ \cancel{1}^{1}\cancel{0}^{,}\,^{1}\cancel{0}\,^{1}\cancel{0}\,^{1}0 \\
-\ 1{,}0\,4\,9 \qquad -\ 1{,}0\ 4\ 9 \\
\hline
8{,}9\ 5\ 1
\end{array}
$$

Here are the steps we followed to solve the problem:

1. Since $0 < 9$, we try to borrow 1 from the tens column, but nothing is there. Since nothing is in the hundreds or thousands column either, we borrow 1 from the ten thousands column to get 0 ten thousands and add 10 to the thousands column to get 10 thousands.

2. We then borrow 1 from the thousands column to get 9 thousands and add 10 to the hundreds column to get 10 hundreds.

3. We borrow 1 from the hundreds column to get 9 hundreds and add 10 to the tens column to get 10 tens.

4. We borrow 1 from the tens column to get 9 tens and add 10 to the ones column to get 10 ones.

5. Now we can do the subtraction, moving from right to left:

$$
10 - 9 = 1 \qquad 9 - 4 = 5 \qquad 9 - 0 = 0 \qquad 9 - 1 = 8
$$

Therefore, you have $8,951 left to deposit into the bank account. Since this is close to our estimate of $9,000, this answer is reasonable. We will now check our answer by adding 8,951 to 1,049 and making sure that the result equals 10,000.

$$
\begin{array}{r}
{\scriptstyle 1\ \ 11} \\
\text{Check:} \qquad 8{,}951 \\
+\ 1{,}049 \\
\hline
10{,}000 \quad \surd \qquad \text{The answer checks.}
\end{array}
$$

Here is a summary of the procedure used to subtract whole numbers.

To Subtract Whole Numbers

1. Write the numbers to be subtracted in a column, lining up digits having the same place value.
2. Subtract the digits in each column, moving from right to left.

3. If a digit in the top number is less than the digit in the same column below it, borrow 1 from the digit to its left and add 10 to that digit.

When you are using this technique, if the digit you need to subtract 1 from is a 0, then subtract 1 from the digit to its left and add 10 to the 0 to get 10. Then subtract 1 from the 10 to get 9, and finally add 10 to the original digit.

MULTIPLICATION OF WHOLE NUMBERS

Multiplication is actually nothing more than repeated addition. For example, multiplying 2 by 10 is the same as adding two 10s; and multiplying 5 by 10 is the same as adding five 10s. Thus, to solve the problem 3×6, we can simply add three 6s to get a result of 18.

$$3 \times 6 = 6 + 6 + 6 = 18$$

Similarly, to multiply 6×3, we simply add six 3s and also obtain a result of 18.

$$6 \times 3 = 3 + 3 + 3 + 3 + 3 + 3 = 18$$

When we multiply numbers, the numbers being multiplied are called **factors,** and the answer is called the **product.** For example, in the equation $7 \times 5 = 35$, the numbers 7 and 5 are called *factors* and 35 is the *product.*

$$
\begin{array}{ccccc}
7 & \times & 5 & = & 35 \\
\uparrow & & \uparrow & & \uparrow \\
\text{factor} & & \text{factor} & & \text{product}
\end{array}
\qquad
\begin{array}{ll}
5 & \text{factor} \\
\times\,7 & \text{factor} \\
\hline
35 & \text{product}
\end{array}
$$

Even though you could eventually figure out the answer to a simple multiplication problem using repeated addition, the process is too time-consuming to be practical. Therefore, it is essential that you memorize all the multiplication tables through 9, and it would be extremely helpful to you if you memorized all the multiplication tables through 12. A copy of the multiplication tables is shown in Figure 3.2.

The answer obtained when any number in the first column is multiplied by any number in the top row is shown in the body of the table. For example, $4 \times 8 = 32$ and $7 \times 12 = 84$. You can create a series of flash cards to help you learn these multiplication facts, or put up signs around your home to remind you of the ones you have the most trouble remembering.

×	0	1	2	3	4	5	6	7	8	9	10	11	12
0	0	0	0	0	0	0	0	0	0	0	0	0	0
1	0	1	2	3	4	5	6	7	8	9	10	11	12
2	0	2	4	6	8	10	12	14	16	18	20	22	24
3	0	3	6	9	12	15	18	21	24	27	30	33	36
4	0	4	8	12	16	20	24	28	32	36	40	44	48
5	0	5	10	15	20	25	30	35	40	45	50	55	60
6	0	6	12	18	24	30	36	42	48	54	60	66	72
7	0	7	14	21	28	35	42	49	56	63	70	77	84
8	0	8	16	24	32	40	48	56	64	72	80	88	96
9	0	9	18	27	36	45	54	63	72	81	90	99	108
10	0	10	20	30	40	50	60	70	80	90	100	110	120
11	0	11	22	33	44	55	66	77	88	99	110	121	132
12	0	12	24	36	48	60	72	84	96	108	120	132	144

Figure 3.2

MULTIPLICATION IN DAILY LIFE: BUYING STOCK

Let us now solve a problem that involves multiplying whole numbers. If a utility stock is selling for $78 a share, how much would it cost to buy 23 shares? To solve this problem, we multiply 78 × 23. We will begin by estimating the answer.

$$78 \approx 80 \quad \text{Since 78 is closer to 80 than to 70}$$
$$\times 23 \approx \times 20 \quad \text{Since 23 is closer to 20 than to 30}$$
$$1,600 \quad 80 \times 20 = 1,600$$

Note that when you multiply numbers that end in zeros, you first multiply the other numbers, ignoring the trailing zeros, and then attach the total number of trailing zeros to your answer. In this case, to multiply 80 × 20, we first multiply 8 × 2 = 16. Since there are a total of two trailing zeros, we attach two zeros to get an estimated cost of $1,600.

To determine the exact answer, we write the problem vertically and multiply each digit in the top number by the ones digit in the bottom number, moving from right to left. We repeat this process for each additional digit in the bottom number, and we write each product under the previous one displaced one column to the left. Finally we add all the products to obtain the final answer.

$$\begin{array}{r} {\scriptstyle 1} \\ {\scriptstyle 2} \\ 78 \\ \times\ 23 \\ \hline 234 \\ 156 \\ \hline 1{,}794 \end{array}$$

$8 \times 3 = 24$. Write down 4, carry 2.

$7 \times 3 = 21$. $21 + 2 = 23$. Write down 23.

$8 \times 2 = 16$. Write down 6, carry 1.

$7 \times 2 = 14$. $14 + 1 = 15$. Write down 15.

Add the two products to obtain 1,794.

The cost of the stock is $1,794. Since this is close to our estimate of $1,600, this answer is reasonable. Here is a summary of the procedure to multiply whole numbers.

To Multiply Whole Numbers

1. Write the numbers to be multiplied in a column with the number having the larger number of digits on top, lining up the ones digits.
2. Multiply each digit in the top number by the ones digit in the bottom number, and write the product below them, starting with the ones digit in the rightmost column.
3. Repeat step 2 for each additional digit in the bottom number, writing each product below the one previously calculated and displaced one column to the left.
4. Add all the products calculated in steps 2 and 3 to obtain the final answer.

Keep in mind that multiplication, like addition, sometimes requires carrying of digits. When we are multiplying numbers using this technique, if the product of any two digits is greater than 9, we write down the digit in the ones place and carry the digit in the tens place one column to the left. We then add this digit to the next product we calculate. This procedure was illustrated in the previous example.

DIVISION OF WHOLE NUMBERS

Division is actually the reverse of multiplication. For example,

$$\text{if}\quad 7 \times 8 = 56 \quad\text{then}\quad 56 \div 8 = 7$$

Therefore, unless you know the multiplication tables so well that you can state the products of single-digit numbers instantaneously, it is almost impossible to do division. Division is also difficult because it is a time-consuming process, and we are more likely to make mistakes. Therefore, it is extremely important that you work slowly and carefully when doing division and to check your work after completing each step.

We will now discuss some of the vocabulary associated with division. When we divide numbers, the number being divided is called the **dividend,** the number we are dividing by is called the **divisor,** and the answer is called the **quotient.** For example, in the equation $28 \div 4 = 7$, 28 is the dividend, 4 is the divisor, and 7 is the quotient. A division problem may be expressed in one of three ways, as shown here:

$$28 \quad \div \quad 4 \quad = \quad 7 \qquad 4\overline{)28} \qquad \frac{28}{4} = 7 \; \leftarrow \text{quotient}$$

quotient ↙

dividend ↙

↑ dividend   ↑ divisor   ↑ quotient   ↗ divisor   ↖ dividend   ↑ divisor

To divide whole numbers, you determine the largest number that can be multiplied by the divisor to produce a product less than or equal to the dividend. Then you subtract that result from the dividend. The number that is left over is called the **remainder.** To check your answer, multiply the quotient by the divisor and add the remainder. The result should equal the dividend.

For example, divide $45 \div 6$ and check your answer as follows.

$$\begin{array}{r} 7\,\text{R}3 \\ 6\overline{)45} \\ -\,42 \\ \hline 3 \end{array}$$

    6 goes into 45 seven times. Write 7 above the dividend.

    Multiply $7 \times 6 = 42$. Subtract $45 - 42 = 3$.

    The remainder is 3.

The answer to the problem is 7 R3, which is read "7 remainder 3." To check that the answer is correct, multiply the quotient (7) by the divisor (6) and add the remainder (3). The result should equal the dividend (45):

$$\text{Check:} \quad \begin{array}{r} 7 \\ \times\,6 \\ \hline 42 \\ +\,3 \\ \hline 45 \quad \surd \end{array}$$

DIVISION IN DAILY LIFE: ROWS IN A LECTURE HALL

Sometimes it takes more than one step to find the quotient. This occurs when the quotient has more than one digit. Such division problems are solved as a series of simpler division problems, by moving from left to right. This is illustrated in the following problem. A lecture hall has 216 seats. If there are 12 seats in each row, how many rows are in the lecture hall? To solve this problem, we divide $216 \div 12$ as follows.

$$\begin{array}{r} 18 \\ 12\overline{\smash{\big)}\,216} \\ -\,12 \\ \hline 96 \\ -\,96 \\ \hline 0 \end{array}$$

12 goes into 21 one time. Write 1 over the 1 in the dividend.

Multiply $12 \times 1 = 12$. Subtract $21 - 12 = 9$.

Bring down the 6 in the dividend.

12 goes into 96 eight times. Write 8 above the 6 in the dividend.

Multiply $12 \times 8 = 96$. Subtract $96 - 96 = 0$.

The remainder is 0.

Therefore, the lecture hall has 18 rows.

$$\text{Check:} \quad \begin{array}{r} 1 \\ 18 \\ \times\,12 \\ \hline 36 \\ 18 \\ \hline 216 \quad \sqrt{} \end{array}$$

DIVISION IN DAILY LIFE: LOTTERY PRIZE

As you solve a division problem, be sure that you write each digit in the quotient, including zeros if appropriate, above the current digit in the dividend. For example, suppose a lottery jackpot of $56,133,035 is to be split equally among 7 lucky winners. How much will each person receive? Let's first estimate the answer. Since $56,133,035 \approx 56,000,000$, which is 56 million, and 56 million $\div\ 7 = 8$ million, our estimate is $8,000,000. We will now determine the exact answer.

$$\begin{array}{r} 8,019,005 \\ 7\overline{\smash{\big)}\,56,133,035} \\ -\,56 \\ \hline 13 \\ -\,7 \\ \hline 63 \\ -\,63 \\ \hline 035 \\ -\,35 \\ \hline 0 \end{array}$$

1. 7 goes into 56 eight times. Write 8 over the 6 in the dividend. $7 \times 8 = 56$. $56 - 56 = 0$. Bring down 1 from the dividend.

2. 7 goes into 1 zero times. Write 0 over the 1 in the dividend. Bring down 3 from the dividend.

3. 7 goes into 13 one time. Write 1 over the 3 in the dividend. $7 \times 1 = 7$. $13 - 7 = 6$. Bring down 3 from the dividend.

4. 7 goes into 63 nine times. Write 9 over the 3 in the dividend. $7 \times 9 = 63$. $63 - 63 = 0$. Bring down 0 from the dividend.

5. 7 goes into 0 zero times. Write 0 over the 0 in the dividend. Bring down 3 from the dividend.

6. 7 goes into 3 zero times. Write 0 over the 3 in the dividend. Bring down 5 from the dividend.

7. 7 goes into 35 five times. Write 5 over the 5 in the dividend. $7 \times 5 = 35$. $35 - 35 = 0$.

Therefore, each winner will receive a prize of $8,019,005. Since this is close to our estimate of $8,000,000, this answer is reasonable. Let's check our answer by multiplying the quotient by the divisor and checking that the result equals the dividend.

$$
\begin{array}{r}
\overset{1\,6\qquad 3}{8{,}019{,}005} \\
\underline{\times\ 7} \\
56{,}133{,}035
\end{array}
$$

Check: 8,019,005 quotient

× 7 divisor

56,133,035 √ dividend

The result is equal to the dividend, so the answer checks.

Here is a summary of the procedure for dividing whole numbers.

To Divide Whole Numbers

1. Write the problem using the *divisor)dividend* format.

2. Find the largest number that can be multiplied by the divisor to obtain a product that is less than or equal to the dividend. This number is called the quotient. Write the quotient above the dividend.

3. Multiply the quotient by the divisor, and subtract the result from the dividend. The number left is called the *remainder*.

To Check a Division Problem

1. Multiply the quotient by the divisor.
2. Add the remainder to the product calculated in step 1.

3. The result should equal the dividend.

WORD PROBLEMS

For many students, just hearing the phrase *word problem* is enough to cause them to experience a major episode of math anxiety. One reason that word problems may seem so overwhelming is that you are so worried about getting the right answer that you do not approach the problem in a methodical way. Developing an effective strategy for tackling the problem is more important than how quickly you can come up with an answer. Since the procedure for solving a word problem may be complicated and lengthy, it is important that you be able to break it down into smaller steps. If you focus on completing one step at a time, you will be less likely to become confused or distracted, and you will make steady progress toward a solution.

The first step in solving any word problem is to read the problem. Do not attempt to absorb all the information presented in the problem the first time that you read it. In fact, during the initial reading you may get no more than a general idea of what the problem is about. Be prepared to reread a problem many times, and each time look for a different piece of information. Pay attention to your thinking process, and focus on details when appropriate.

Don't panic when you think that you have reached a dead end and you don't know what to do next. Often, eliminating the strategies that do not work will narrow down the possibilities and can help lead you to the ones that do result in a solution. If you become frustrated, you can always start over with a fresh approach.

If you are having trouble visualizing what you are being asked to do, draw a diagram and label it with the specific pieces of information presented in the problem. Sometimes, simply listing the quantities that are known can help jump-start your thinking process so that it becomes clear how to find the quantities that are unknown.

Finally, do not become fixated on finding the "right way" to solve the problem. There are many ways to solve many problems, and one method is not necessarily better than another. However, once you have analyzed a problem and decided upon a particular strategy, don't switch to another plan of action unless you are willing to start over from the beginning. Here is a summary of the methods we have discussed to help you succeed with word problems.

Ways to Win with Word Problems

1. Develop a step-by-step approach.
2. Reread the problem as many times as necessary to gather all critical information.
3. Don't panic when a strategy fails. Simply try another approach.
4. Draw diagrams or make lists to help you understand the problem.
5. Acknowledge that there are many ways to solve a problem.

WORD PROBLEMS IN DAILY LIFE: SALES PROFITS

Let us now apply these techniques for solving word problems to a practical example. An electronics store bought 80 cameras at a cost of $60 apiece. The cameras were then sold at four different prices. If 18 sold at $120, 37 sold at $100, 11 sold at $85, and 14 sold at $80, how much profit did the store make on the sale of these cameras? The first time you read this problem you may be overwhelmed by all the information presented, and you may not remember much except the fact that the problem is about cameras. However, on the next reading, you should be able to determine what you are asked to find, which is the profit on the sale of the cameras. We will now develop a strategy to solve the problem. Since profit is sales revenue minus cost, we need to find the sales revenue and the cost of the cameras. Here are the steps we will use to solve the problem:

1. Find the total cost by multiplying the number of cameras by the cost per camera.
2. Find the sales revenue at each price by multiplying the number of cameras sold by the price.
3. Find the total sales revenue by adding the sales revenues calculated at each price.
4. Find the profit by subtracting the total cost from the total sales revenue.

To complete each step, we will need to reread the problem to find a particular piece of information.

1. Total cost = # Cameras × Cost per camera
   Total cost = 80 × $60 = $4,800

2. Sales revenue = # Cameras × Price per camera
   Sales revenue at $120 = 18 × $120 = $2,160
   Sales revenue at $100 = 37 × $100 = 3,700
   Sales revenue at $85 = 11 × $85 =   935
   Sales revenue at $80 = 14 × $80 = 1,120

3. Total sales revenue: $7,915

4. Total sales revenue: $7,915
   Total cost: − 4,800
   Profit: $3,115

Therefore, the store had a profit of $3,115.

1. Calculate the total cost by multiplying the number of cameras by cost per camera.
2. Calculate the sales revenue at each price by multiplying the number of cameras sold at each of the four different prices by the price.
3. Calculate the total sales revenue by adding the sales revenues at each price.
4. Calculate the profit by subtracting the total cost from the total sales revenue.

 ## STRATEGIES FOR SUCCESS

Now that we have reviewed the techniques for performing basic operations on whole numbers, you probably have a better idea of what to do with problems that require you to add, subtract, multiply, and divide. Although mathematics has a lot of terminology to describe how to work with numbers, hopefully you will be less intimidated by it, and you will learn the meaning of words that you do not understand. You should also recognize why memorizing the multiplication tables is a critical component to mastering basic math skills. Also, when you are performing complicated operations such as long division, be sure to work slowly and carefully, and check your work after every step to avoid careless mistakes. Finally, don't panic when you encounter a word problem. Instead, take a methodical approach, and work through the problem one step at a time. Here is a summary of the strategies for "becoming nimble with numbers."

STRATEGIES FOR SUCCESS WITH WHOLE NUMBERS

1. Review the techniques for addition, subtraction, multiplication, and division.
2. Learn the meaning of the terminology used in mathematics.
3. Memorize the multiplication tables through 12.
4. Work slowly and carefully, and check your work after every step.
5. Use a methodical approach to solving word problems.

CHAPTER 3 EXERCISES

1. Learn the multiplication facts up to 12 × 12. Write down the ones you have trouble remembering. Post them in a prominent location that you look at every day.
2. Explain in your own words how to use borrowing to subtract one number from another. Give an example that illustrates this procedure.
3. Pick a page in a magazine that contains mostly text, and estimate the number of words on that page. Explain the process you used to arrive at your estimate.

4

Fighting Fear of Fractions

MATH MEMORIES

"I was traumatized in school by fractions. The teacher made me solve a problem at the board and ridiculed me in front of the entire class. Everyone laughed at me, and since then I have had a mental block with math."

"I never really understood fractions. I relied on using all kinds of tricks I memorized, but they did not work all the time."

"I could do fractions, as long as I remembered the rules and the problems were simple. But whenever I could not get the answer right away, I got lost and could not regain my confidence."

"I never thought I needed to learn math, because I was never interested in careers that required it. But now I want to become a carpenter, and you need to work with fractions all the time."

"I work in a fabric store, and I am amazed at how many people can't figure out how many yards of material they need because they don't understand fractions."

COMMON PROBLEMS

Fractions have always been a major stumbling block for students. There are a number of reasons why this is so. First, the terminology is difficult to remember. There are a lot of words associated with fractions such as *numerator, denominator, proper, improper, factor,* and *reciprocal,* and it is important to know the precise meaning of each in order to be able to work with fractions effectively.

Students also have trouble with fractions because students do not know the multiplication tables well. Unless you can quickly call to mind common multiplication facts, such as 56 is equal to 7 times 8, you will find operations with fractions to be very difficult and time-consuming.

Since children learn about fractions at an early age, adults often feel that they are stupid if they cannot remember how to add or subtract fractions. Actually, operations involving fractions require some of the most complicated mathematical techniques in all of arithmetic. If you have not practiced applying these techniques in a long time, it is easy to forget them.

We also have trouble working with fractions because the solution of many types of problems involves applying multistep techniques. If you do not have a clear understanding of how each step leads to the next, it is easy to get lost and be unable to solve the problem. For example, the process of adding two fractions may involve as many as four different steps. If you do not understand how to perform any of these steps, or if at a certain point you forget what to do next, it is impossible to obtain the correct answer.

Another common problem in working with fractions involves careless mistakes. Since you can do operations such as multiplication and division very quickly, it is very tempting to rush through a problem without checking your work.

HINTS FOR STUDYING FRACTIONS

Before you begin your study of fractions, take some time to learn the meaning of the words used to describe them. Even though some words such as *numerator* and *denominator* pertain only to fractions, other words such as *factor* and *improper* may have other meanings and may sound familiar to you. Don't fool yourself into thinking that you understand the mathematical meaning of words whose meaning you understand in a nonmathematical context. If you do not understand exactly how a particular word is used to describe how to do a mathematical operation on fractions, look it up. Use more than one book if necessary, and read as many explanations as you need to fully understand the concept.

It is essential that you memorize all the multiplication tables through 9, and it would be extremely valuable to learn 10, 11, and 12 as well. The multiplication table shown in Figure 3.2 can be used as a starting point. Once you can quickly remember the answer to any multiplication problem from this table, it will be much easier for you to work not only with fractions, but also with other mathematical subjects, such as algebra.

The only way you will become comfortable working with fractions is to do a lot of problems. Many techniques will seem very complicated at first, and the more you practice, the easier it will be for you to remember what to do. Begin with simpler problems, and once you master them, move on to more difficult ones. You need to do a lot of problems to build up both confidence and speed. Even though we see fractions a lot, we often try to avoid doing a lot of calculations with fractions in daily life. That is why we usually forget the various techniques, and are at a loss as to what to do when we encounter a problem that requires us to work with fractions.

When you are working with multistep problems involving fractions, it is often helpful to write down a stepwise strategy for solving the problem. As you complete each step, mark it as complete, and then move on to the next one. If you have difficulty remembering how to solve a particular type of problem because the numbers are too large, think of a simple problem first, to help you remember the technique.

To avoid common mistakes in working with fractions, work slowly and carefully and clearly show all your work. Errors are often likely to be made when we multiply or divide fractions, and when we reduce fractions to lowest terms. Whenever you are working on a problem that involves many steps, check each step before moving on to the next one, so that you do not end up redoing the entire problem if you find that you have made a mistake.

WHAT IS A FRACTION?

We will begin our formal study of fractions by defining some of the common terms associated with them. A fraction is used to represent parts of a whole. The **numerator** is the top number in a fraction, and the **denominator** is the bottom number.

Figure 4.1 illustrates the meaning of a fraction. It represents a whole circle divided into 3 equal parts. Since 1 out of 3 parts of the whole circle is shaded, this diagram represents the fraction $\frac{1}{3}$. The top number, 1, is called the numerator, and it represents the number of parts being considered. The bottom number, 3, is called the denominator, and it represents the total number of equal parts into which the whole is divided.

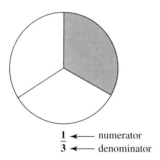

$$\frac{1}{3} \longleftarrow \text{numerator} \atop \longleftarrow \text{denominator}$$

Figure 4.1

The fraction $\frac{1}{3}$ is read as "one-third." The names of some other fractions are shown here.

$$\frac{2}{5} \qquad \text{two-fifths}$$

$$\frac{17}{20} \qquad \text{seventeen-twentieths}$$

$$\frac{36}{49} \qquad \text{thirty-six forty-ninths}$$

$$\frac{51}{100} \qquad \text{fifty-one hundredths}$$

PROPERTIES OF FRACTIONS

A fraction is another way of expressing the operation division. For example, the fraction $\frac{20}{5}$ means $20 \div 5$, which is equal to the number 4. Similarly,

$$\frac{54}{6} = 54 \div 6 = 9$$

Fractions in which the numerators are equal to the denominators are equal to 1. For example, the fractions $\frac{3}{3}, \frac{16}{16}$, and $\frac{127}{127}$ are all equal to 1. We can use the fact that a fraction represents the operation division to illustrate this.

$$\frac{3}{3} = 3 \div 3 = 1$$

$$\frac{16}{16} = 16 \div 16 = 1$$

$$\frac{127}{127} = 127 \div 127 = 1$$

We can also represent the fractions $\frac{3}{3}, \frac{5}{5}$, and $\frac{8}{8}$ by the diagrams shown in Figure 4.2. Notice that in each case, the entire circle, or 1 circle, is shaded. Thus, $\frac{3}{3}, \frac{5}{5}$, and $\frac{8}{8}$ are all equal to 1.

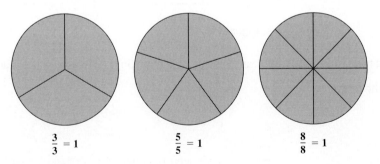

$$\frac{3}{3} = 1 \qquad\qquad \frac{5}{5} = 1 \qquad\qquad \frac{8}{8} = 1$$

Figure 4.2

Fractions in which the denominators are 1 are equal to the numerators. For example, the fraction $\frac{9}{1}$ is equal to 9 since $9 \div 1 = 9$. Therefore, any whole number can be written as a fraction with a denominator of 1. Consider these examples:

$$34 = \frac{34}{1} \qquad \text{since} \qquad \frac{34}{1} = 34 \div 1 = 34$$

$$286 = \frac{286}{1} \qquad \text{since} \qquad \frac{286}{1} = 286 \div 1 = 286$$

Fractions that have a numerator of 0 are equal to 0. For example, the fraction $\frac{0}{14}$ is equal to 0 since

$$\frac{0}{14} = 0 \div 14 = 0$$

Fractions having a denominator of 0 are said to be **undefined** since division by 0 is impossible. Therefore, the fraction $\frac{7}{0}$ is undefined, or has no meaning, since it is not possible to divide the number 7 by 0.

TYPES OF FRACTIONS

A **proper fraction** is a fraction whose numerator is less than its denominator. For example, the fractions $\frac{1}{3}, \frac{7}{8}$, and $\frac{19}{47}$ are all proper fractions. Looking back at Figure 4.1, which represents the fraction $\frac{1}{3}$, we can see that 1 out of 3 parts of the circle is shaded, which is less than the whole circle. Therefore, a proper fraction represents a value less than 1.

An **improper fraction** is a fraction whose numerator is greater than or equal to its denominator. For example, the fractions $\frac{3}{2}, \frac{9}{4}, \frac{7}{7}$, and $\frac{27}{3}$ are all improper fractions. Improper fractions represent values greater than or equal to 1. For example, the improper fraction $\frac{9}{4}$ can be represented by the diagram shown in Figure 4.3, in which a series of circles are each divided into 4 pieces, and 9 of these pieces are shaded. Notice that we could also describe this diagram by saying that $2\frac{1}{4}$ pieces are shaded. Therefore, the fraction $\frac{9}{4}$ is equal to $2\frac{1}{4}$. The number $2\frac{1}{4}$ is a mixed number, which is the sum of the whole number 2 and the fraction $\frac{1}{4}$. A **mixed number** is the sum of a whole number and a fraction.

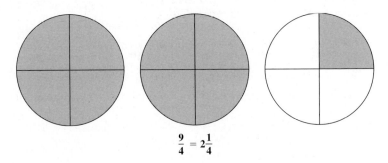

$$\frac{9}{4} = 2\frac{1}{4}$$

Figure 4.3

The relationship between improper fractions and their representations as mixed numbers can be shown by the diagram in Figure 4.4, in which a line is divided into equal segments so that the size of each piece can be represented by the fraction $\frac{1}{4}$.

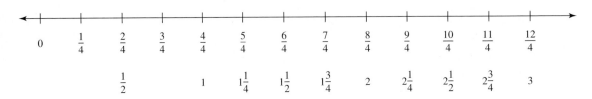

Figure 4.4

Notice that an improper fraction can represent either a whole number greater than or equal to 1, or a mixed number, which includes a fractional part. For example, $\frac{4}{4} = 1$, $\frac{8}{4} = 2$, and $\frac{11}{4} = 2\frac{3}{4}$.

In daily living situations, we use the mixed number representation rather than the improper fraction. For example, we might say that we live $2\frac{3}{4}$ miles from work, or that a recipe requires $1\frac{1}{2}$ cups of sugar. However, the improper fraction representation is important for many mathematical operations, such as multiplication and division of fractions, and for working with fractions in solving algebraic equations. Since different forms of fractions are used for different purposes, it is important to be able to convert from one form to another.

CONVERTING BETWEEN MIXED NUMBERS AND IMPROPER FRACTIONS

We now discuss the procedures for converting mixed numbers to improper fractions and improper fractions to mixed numbers.

To Convert a Mixed Number to an Improper Fraction

1. Multiply the whole number part by the denominator of the fractional part.

2. Add the numerator.

3. Place the result over the denominator of the fractional part.

We will now convert $2\frac{3}{4}$ to an improper fraction, following this procedure.

$2 \times 4 = 8$ Multiply the whole number part, 2, by the denominator of the fractional part, 4, to get 8.

$8 + 3 = 11$ Add the numerator, 3, to 8 to obtain 11.

$2\frac{3}{4} = \frac{11}{4}$ Place the result, 11, over the denominator of the fractional part, 4.

The equivalent improper fraction is $\frac{11}{4}$. We can write this procedure in one line like this:

$$2\frac{3}{4} = \frac{2 \times 4 + 3}{4} = \frac{8 + 3}{4} = \frac{11}{4}$$

Looking at Figure 4.5, we can see that this procedure is the same as finding the total number of shaded parts in all the circles displayed. We first multiply

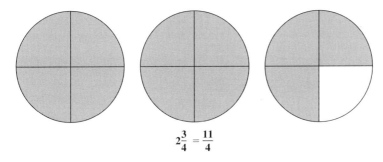

$$2\frac{3}{4} = \frac{11}{4}$$

Figure 4.5

the 2 completely shaded circles by the number of parts in each circle, 4, to obtain a total of 8 shaded parts. We then add the 3 additional shaded parts in the last circle to obtain a total of 11 shaded parts.

Here are some additional examples of converting mixed numbers to improper fractions.

$$5\frac{7}{8} = \frac{5 \times 8 + 7}{8} = \frac{40 + 7}{8} = \frac{47}{8}$$

$$12\frac{2}{5} = \frac{12 \times 5 + 2}{5} = \frac{60 + 2}{5} = \frac{62}{5}$$

To convert an improper fraction to a mixed number, we simply need to remember that a fraction represents the operation division. Here is the procedure.

To Convert an Improper Fraction to a Mixed Number

1. Divide the numerator by the denominator.
2. The resulting number, or quotient, is the whole number part of the mixed number.

3. The remainder over the denominator is the fractional part of the mixed number. If the remainder is 0, the improper fraction is equal to a whole number.

For example, we can convert $\frac{17}{3}$ to a mixed number as follows.

$$\frac{17}{3} = 17 \div 3 = 5\,R\,2 \qquad$$ Divide 17 by 3. The answer is 5 with a remainder of 2, or 5 R 2.

The whole number portion is the quotient, 5.

The fractional portion is the remainder over the denominator, $\frac{2}{3}$.

The resulting mixed number is $5\frac{2}{3}$.

Therefore, $\frac{17}{3} = 5\frac{2}{3}$.

Notice that the fraction $\frac{17}{3}$ is simply another way to express the division problem $17 \div 3$. This is true for other fractions as well, as long as the denominator is not equal to 0.

Here are some additional examples using this technique:

$$\frac{56}{8} = 56 \div 8 = 7$$

$$\frac{125}{5} = 125 \div 5 = 25$$

$$\frac{37}{9} = 37 \div 9 = 4 \text{ R } 1 = 4\frac{1}{9}$$

$$\frac{259}{8} = 259 \div 8 = 32 \text{ R } 3 = 32\frac{3}{8}$$

EQUIVALENT FRACTIONS

Fractions that have the same value can be represented in a number of different ways. For example, the fraction $\frac{1}{2}$ can also be represented as $\frac{2}{4}$ or $\frac{3}{6}$, as shown in Figure 4.6.

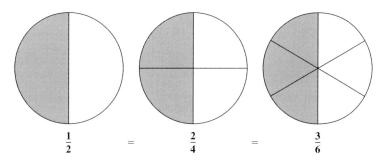

Figure 4.6

Notice that when the circle is cut into 4 equal parts, we can represent one-half of the circle by shading 2 out of its 4 pieces. When the circle is cut into 6 equal parts, we can represent one-half of the circle by shading 3 out of its 6 pieces.

Equivalent fractions are fractions that have the same value. The following fractions are also examples of equivalent fractions, as illustrated in Figure 4.7.

$$\frac{1}{3} = \frac{3}{9} = \frac{4}{12}$$

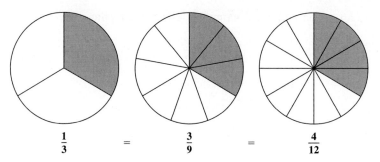

Figure 4.7

Sometimes it is necessary to convert a fraction to an equivalent fraction that has the same value, but has a different denominator that may be larger or smaller than the original fraction. This is done by using the following procedure:

To Convert a Fraction to an Equivalent Fraction

Multiply or divide both the numerator and the denominator by the same nonzero number.

For example, to convert the fraction $\dfrac{3}{4}$ to an equivalent fraction with a denominator of 20, we first ask ourselves, What number must 4 be multiplied by to obtain 20?

$$\frac{3}{4} = \frac{?}{20}$$

Since $4 \times 5 = 20$, we can then multiply both numerator and denominator by 5 to obtain an equivalent fraction with a denominator of 20. We multiply 3×5 to find the missing numerator:

$$\frac{3}{4} = \frac{3 \times 5}{4 \times 5} = \frac{15}{20}$$

Therefore, the equivalent fraction is $\dfrac{15}{20}$.

Recall that when we multiply the numerator and denominator by the same nonzero number, we are actually multiplying the fraction by the number 1.

$$\frac{3 \times 5}{4 \times 5} = \frac{3}{4} \times \frac{5}{5} = \frac{3}{4} \times 1$$

Therefore, the resulting equivalent fraction has the same value as the original fraction.

REDUCING TO LOWEST TERMS

Sometimes we are asked to reduce a fraction to lowest terms. A fraction is in **lowest terms** if both the numerator and the denominator cannot be divided by any number greater than 1. For example, the fraction $\dfrac{21}{56}$ is not in lowest terms because both the numerator and the denominator can be divided by 7.

$$\frac{21}{56} = \frac{21 \div 7}{56 \div 7} = \frac{3}{8}$$

Notice that the resulting fraction, $\dfrac{3}{8}$, is in lowest terms. When working with fractions, we express the answers as fractions reduced to lowest terms because they are the simplest form for fractions having the same value.

To Reduce a Fraction to Lowest Terms

1. Find the largest number by which both the numerator and the denominator are divisible.

2. Divide both the numerator and the denominator by that number.

When you are reducing fractions, if you cannot determine the largest number by which both the numerator and the denominator are divisible, just divide the numerator and denominator by a series of numbers until the resulting fraction is in lowest terms. For example, you could reduce the fraction $\dfrac{36}{48}$ to lowest terms in either of the following ways:

$$\frac{36}{48} = \frac{36 \div 12}{48 \div 12} = \frac{3}{4}$$

$$\frac{36}{48} = \frac{36 \div 2}{48 \div 2} = \frac{18}{24} = \frac{18 \div 3}{24 \div 3} = \frac{6}{8} = \frac{6 \div 2}{8 \div 2} = \frac{3}{4}$$

The number 12 is said to be the greatest common factor of 36 and 48 because it is the largest number by which both 36 and 48 are divisible. The **greatest common factor,** or **GCF,** of two or more numbers is the largest number by which each of the given numbers is divisible. The numbers 2 and 3 are also common factors of 36 and 48, but neither one is the greatest common factor.

We can also show this process of dividing both numerator and denominator by a series of common factors by crossing out each number as it is divided by each common factor. This process is called **canceling.** For example, we can reduce $\dfrac{30}{45}$ to lowest terms as illustrated here.

$$
\begin{array}{cc}
\overset{2}{\cancel{6}} & \text{Divide by 3.} \\
\cancel{30} & \text{Divide by 5.} \\
\overline{\cancel{45}} & \text{Divide by 5.} \\
\underset{3}{\cancel{9}} & \text{Divide by 3.}
\end{array}
$$

Therefore, $\dfrac{30}{45} = \dfrac{2}{3}$

LOWEST COMMON DENOMINATOR

It is often necessary to rewrite fractions so that they have the same denominator. This is important because it enables us to compare the size of fractions and to add and subtract them.

For example, it is difficult to determine which distance is greater, $\dfrac{2}{3}$ mile or $\dfrac{5}{8}$ mile, because the denominators 3 and 8 are different. However, if we convert each fraction to an equivalent fraction with the same denominator, it will be easier to compare them. To do this, we first find the lowest common denominator, or LCD, of 3 and 8. One way to find a common denominator (but not necessarily the lowest) is to multiply the two denominators. In this case, since $3 \times 8 = 24$, 24 is a common denominator. The **lowest common denominator (LCD)** is the smallest number that is divisible by each of the original denominators. Since 24 is the smallest number that is divisible by both 3 and 8, it is also the lowest common denominator.

Now let us go back to our original problem of determining which distance is greater, $\dfrac{2}{3}$ mile or $\dfrac{5}{8}$ mile. We have already determined that the LCD of $\dfrac{2}{3}$ and $\dfrac{5}{8}$ is 24. Now we will convert $\dfrac{2}{3}$ and $\dfrac{5}{8}$ to equivalent fractions with a denominator of 24:

$$\frac{2}{3} = \frac{?}{24}$$

$$\frac{5}{8} = \frac{?}{24}$$

We need to find the missing numerator in each of the equivalent fractions. To find an equivalent fraction to $\dfrac{2}{3}$ with a denominator of 24, we multiply both numerator and denominator by 8:

$$\frac{2}{3} = \frac{2 \times 8}{3 \times 8} = \frac{16}{24}$$

Similarly, to find an equivalent fraction to $\frac{5}{8}$ with a denominator of 24, we multiply both numerator and denominator by 3:

$$\frac{5}{8} = \frac{5 \times 3}{8 \times 3} = \frac{15}{24}$$

We can now compare the two fractions that have a denominator of 24. When the denominators are the same, the larger fraction is the fraction with the larger numerator.

$$\text{Since} \quad \frac{16}{24} > \frac{15}{24} \quad \text{and} \quad \frac{2}{3} = \frac{16}{24} \quad \text{and} \quad \frac{5}{8} = \frac{15}{24}$$

we can conclude that $\frac{2}{3} > \frac{5}{8}$. Therefore, $\frac{2}{3}$ mile is a greater distance than $\frac{5}{8}$ mile.

Let's consider another example. To find a common denominator of the fractions $\frac{5}{6}$ and $\frac{2}{9}$, we could also multiply the two denominators, 6×9, to obtain 54. However, 54 is not the smallest number by which 6 and 9 are divisible. To find the lowest common denominator, we could list all the numbers obtained when 6 and 9 are multiplied by $1, 2, 3, 4, 5, 6$, etc. These numbers are called multiples. A **multiple** of a given number is the number obtained when the given number is multiplied by another number. The smallest number that appears in both lists, that is, the smallest number that is a multiple of both 6 and 9, is the LCD. The first five multiples of 6 and 9 are listed here:

$$6: \qquad 6, 12, \enclose{circle}{18}, 24, 30, \ldots$$
$$9: \qquad 9, \enclose{circle}{18}, 27, 36, 45, \ldots$$

The smallest number that appears in both lists is 18. Therefore, the LCD of $\frac{5}{6}$ and $\frac{2}{9}$ is 18. We will now summarize the procedure for finding the LCD:

To Find the Lowest Common Denominator (LCD) of Two or More Fractions

1. List the first few multiples of each denominator until the same number appears in each list.

2. The LCD is the smallest number that appears in both lists.

For example, to find the LCD of $\frac{5}{12}$ and $\frac{7}{8}$, we list the multiples of 12 and 8:

$$12: \quad 12, \boxed{24}, 36, 48, 60, 72, \ldots$$
$$8: \quad 8, 16, \boxed{24}, 32, 40, 48, \ldots$$

The LCD of $\frac{5}{12}$ and $\frac{7}{8}$ is 24 because it is the smallest number in both lists. Notice that 48 is also a common denominator, since it appears in both lists. But it is not the *lowest* common denominator.

By now you can begin to see the importance of learning the multiplication tables thoroughly so that you are able to work with fractions easily. Don't become discouraged if it takes you a while to feel confident with all the terminology and techniques. Given the right amount of time, effort, and practice, fractions will become easier.

ADDITION AND SUBTRACTION OF FRACTIONS

We will now look at some examples of how fractions might be used to solve problems in daily life. Many situations that involve comparisons or measurements do require the use of fractions. It is also useful to develop the skills needed to do basic operations on fractions, since these skills will help you understand other concepts, such as decimals and percents, that also arise frequently in daily life.

Addition and subtraction of fractions are probably the most difficult operations because they require many steps to find the answer. Consider this example. If $\frac{1}{2}$ of one pie and $\frac{1}{3}$ of another pie are left uneaten, what is the total amount of pie left over? To solve this problem, we need to add the fractions $\frac{1}{2} + \frac{1}{3}$. This is illustrated in Figure 4.8.

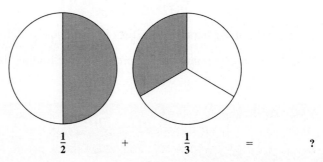

$$\frac{1}{2} \qquad + \qquad \frac{1}{3} \qquad = \qquad ?$$

Figure 4.8

It would be easier to solve this problem if both pies were cut into the same number of pieces, that is, if both fractions had the same denominator. We therefore need to find the LCD of $\frac{1}{2}$ and $\frac{1}{3}$. To this, we list a few multiples of 2 and 3:

$$2: \quad 2, 4, \textcircled{6}, 8, \ldots$$
$$3: \quad 3, \textcircled{6}, 9, 12, \ldots$$

Since the smallest number in both lists is 6, the LCD of $\frac{1}{2}$ and $\frac{1}{3}$ is 6.

$$\frac{1}{2} = \frac{1 \times 3}{2 \times 3} = \frac{3}{6} \qquad \frac{1}{3} = \frac{1 \times 2}{3 \times 2} = \frac{2}{6}$$

We can now redraw our pies, showing each pie cut into 6 pieces.

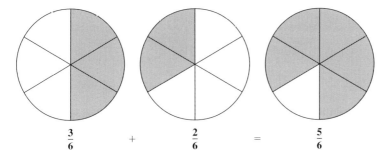

$$\frac{3}{6} \qquad + \qquad \frac{2}{6} \qquad = \qquad \frac{5}{6}$$

Figure 4.9

From Figure 4.9, we can see that

$$\frac{1}{2} + \frac{1}{3} = \frac{3}{6} + \frac{2}{6} = \frac{5}{6}$$

Therefore, to add or subtract fractions, we can use the following procedure:

To Add or Subtract Fractions

1. Find the lowest common denominator (LCD) of each fraction.
2. Change each fraction to an equivalent fraction with a denominator equal to the LCD.
3. Add or subtract the numerators, and place the result over the common denominator.

We will now illustrate the procedure for subtracting mixed numbers. Consider this example. Suppose you live 4 miles from work. If you stop for gas $1\frac{3}{4}$ miles away from home, how much farther must you travel to get to work? To solve this problem, we subtract $4 - 1\frac{3}{4}$ as illustrated in Figure 4.10. Of the 4 circles displayed, $1\frac{3}{4}$ are shaded, leaving $2\frac{1}{4}$ circles that are not shaded. Therefore, $4 - 1\frac{3}{4} = 2\frac{1}{4}$.

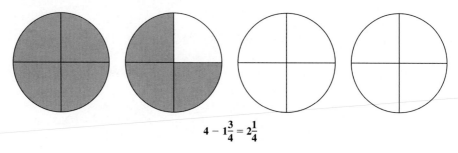

$$4 - 1\tfrac{3}{4} = 2\tfrac{1}{4}$$

Figure 4.10

To subtract mixed numbers mathematically, we subtract the whole number and fractional parts separately. Since the number 4 has no fractional part, we rewrite it as follows:

$$4 = 3 + 1 = 3 + \frac{4}{4} = 3\frac{4}{4}$$

We can rewrite 1 as the fraction $\frac{4}{4}$, since 4 is the denominator of the fractional part of the number we wish to subtract, which is $1\frac{3}{4}$. It is often easiest to write problems involving addition and subtraction of fractions vertically, as shown here:

$$4 = 3 + 1 = \quad 3\frac{4}{4} \qquad \text{Subtract the whole numbers: } 3 - 1 = 2$$

$$-1\frac{3}{4} = -1\frac{3}{4} = -1\frac{3}{4} \qquad \text{Subtract the fractional parts: } \frac{4}{4} - \frac{3}{4} = \frac{1}{4}$$

$$\overline{\qquad\qquad\qquad 2\frac{1}{4}}$$

Therefore, you must travel an additional $2\frac{1}{4}$ miles to get to work.

Addition of mixed numbers is similar to subtraction, since you add the whole number and fractional parts separately.

We will now summarize the procedure for adding and subtracting mixed numbers.

To Add or Subtract Mixed Numbers

1. Convert the fractional parts to equivalent fractions with the same denominator.

2. Add or subtract the whole number and fractional parts separately.

3. In subtracting mixed numbers, if the fractional portion of the first number is less than the fractional portion of the second number, rewrite the first number by subtracting 1 from the whole number part and adding 1 to the fractional part.

As mentioned earlier, addition and subtraction are the hardest operations to perform on fractions because they involve so many steps. Subtraction of mixed numbers can be especially difficult if you need to rewrite the first number in order to subtract the fractional parts. As you shall see, multiplication and division of fractions are somewhat easier.

MULTIPLICATION OF FRACTIONS

Multiplication of fractions can be illustrated by the diagram in Figure 4.11. Suppose you had $\frac{1}{3}$ of a pie remaining and you ate $\frac{1}{2}$ of what was left. What fraction of the total pie would you have eaten?

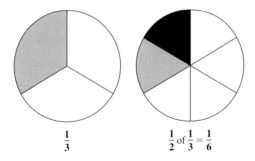

$$\frac{1}{3} \qquad \frac{1}{2} \text{ of } \frac{1}{3} = \frac{1}{6}$$

Figure 4.11

The problem asks you to find $\frac{1}{2}$ of $\frac{1}{3}$. From Figure 4.11, you can see that $\frac{1}{2}$ of $\frac{1}{3} = \frac{1}{6}$. In working with fractions, the word *of* means to multiply. Therefore, to multiply fractions, simply multiply the numerators and multiply the denominators.

$$\frac{1}{2} \text{ of } \frac{1}{3} = \frac{1}{2} \times \frac{1}{3} \qquad \text{The word } of \text{ means to multiply.}$$

$$= \frac{1 \times 1}{2 \times 3} \qquad \text{Multiply the numerators. Multiply the denominators.}$$

$$= \frac{1}{6}$$

Let us look at another example involving mixed numbers. Suppose a cookie recipe requires $2\frac{3}{4}$ cups of flour. How much flour is required to double the recipe? To solve this problem, you need to multiply:

$$2\frac{3}{4} \times 2$$

Since this is a somewhat complicated problem involving many steps, you should first estimate what an appropriate answer might be. If your final answer is not close to your estimate, you know that you made a mistake in the calculation or in the estimate.

To estimate the answer to our problem, use the approximation $2\frac{3}{4} \approx 3$. The symbol $\approx$ means "approximately equal to." To double a recipe requiring 3 cups of flour, you need 6 cups of flour. Your final answer therefore should be close to 6.

To find the exact answer, first you need to change both numbers being multiplied to improper fractions. Then you can multiply those fractions by multiplying the numerators and the denominators. Finally, convert the result to a mixed number, so that it makes sense. This procedure is shown here.

$$2\frac{3}{4} = \frac{2 \times 4 + 3}{4} = \frac{8 + 3}{4} = \frac{11}{4} \qquad \text{and} \qquad 2 = \frac{2}{1} \qquad \begin{array}{l}\text{Change each number to}\\ \text{an improper fraction.}\end{array}$$

$$2\frac{3}{4} \times 2 = \frac{11}{4} \times \frac{2}{1} \qquad \text{Multiply the two improper fractions.}$$

$$= \frac{11 \times 2}{4 \times 1} \qquad \text{Multiply the numerators. Multiply the denominators.}$$

$$= \frac{22}{4} \qquad \text{It is hard to imagine how much flour this represents.}$$

$$\frac{22}{4} = 22 \div 4$$

Convert to a mixed number by dividing the numerator by the denominator.

$$= 5 \text{ R } 2$$

The quotient is 5, and the remainder is 2.

$$= 5\frac{2}{4}$$

The whole number part is 5; the fractional part is $\frac{2}{4}$.

$$= 5\frac{1}{2}$$

Reduce the fractional part to lowest terms.

Therefore, to double the recipe requires $5\frac{1}{2}$ cups of flour. Since $5\frac{1}{2}$ is close to our estimate of 6, this answer is reasonable.

We will now summarize the procedure for multiplying fractions and mixed numbers.

To Multiply Fractions and Mixed Numbers

1. Change each mixed number to an improper fraction.
2. Multiply the numerators to obtain the numerator of the answer.
3. Multiply the denominators to obtain the denominator of the answer.
4. If appropriate, change the resulting fraction to a mixed number.
5. If necessary, reduce to lowest terms.

DIVISION OF FRACTIONS

To illustrate the division of fractions, consider the following problem. Suppose you have $\frac{1}{2}$ of a pie remaining and you want to divide it into 5 equal pieces. How large will each piece be? The problem to be solved is $\frac{1}{2} \div 5$. From Figure 4.12, we can see that $\frac{1}{2} \div 5 = \frac{1}{10}$.

Notice that this result can be obtained by multiplying $\frac{1}{2}$ by the fraction $\frac{1}{5}$.

$$\frac{1}{2} \div 5 = \frac{1}{2} \cdot \frac{1}{5} = \frac{1}{10}$$

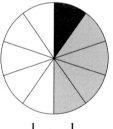

$\frac{1}{2} \div 5 = \frac{1}{10}$

Figure 4.12

Since $5 = \frac{5}{1}$, the fraction $\frac{1}{5}$ is obtained by switching the numerator and denominator of the fraction $\frac{5}{1}$. And so $\frac{1}{5}$ is said to be the reciprocal of 5. The

reciprocal of a fraction is obtained by switching the numerator and the denominator. Some examples of fractions and their reciprocals are shown here:

Fraction	Reciprocal
$\dfrac{3}{8}$	$\dfrac{8}{3}$
$\dfrac{51}{17}$	$\dfrac{17}{51}$
$\dfrac{1}{25}$	25
63	$\dfrac{1}{63}$
$6\dfrac{2}{7} = \dfrac{44}{7}$	$\dfrac{7}{44}$

Therefore, to divide two fractions, we multiply the first fraction by the reciprocal of the second.

$$\frac{1}{2} \div 5 = \frac{1}{2} \div \frac{5}{1} = \frac{1}{2} \cdot \frac{1}{5} = \frac{1}{10}$$

We will now summarize the procedure for dividing fractions and mixed numbers.

To Divide Fractions and Mixed Numbers

1. Change each mixed number to an improper fraction.
2. Multiply the first fraction by the reciprocal of the second fraction.
3. If appropriate, change the resulting fraction to a mixed number.
4. If necessary, reduce to lowest terms.

Multiplication and division of fractions can often be done more quickly than addition and subtraction of fractions. Because of this, we are likely to rush through a problem and make careless mistakes. It is therefore important that we estimate answers whenever possible and work slowly and carefully, checking each step, as we solve a problem.

There are now a few calculators available that allow us to enter mixed numbers and fractions and then display answers in that format. It is more awkward to use a calculator with fractions than with other numbers, but since operations on fractions can be time-consuming, it might be worth the effort. If you do use a calculator to solve problems with fractions, be certain to estimate your answer before pressing the keys, and always check that your answer is reasonable.

FRACTIONS IN DAILY LIFE: MOVING FURNITURE

We will now draw on our knowledge of fractions to solve some additional problems using fractions. A desk that is $39\frac{5}{8}$ inches long is moved against a wall that measures $76\frac{1}{2}$ inches in length. How much space is left along that wall for a filing cabinet? To solve this problem, we need to subtract $76\frac{1}{2} - 39\frac{5}{8}$. Before we solve the problem, we will estimate the answer by approximating the two fractions and finding their difference as shown here:

$$76\frac{1}{2} \approx 77$$

$$39\frac{5}{8} \approx 40$$

$$77 - 40 = 37$$

Therefore, the answer should be close to 37 inches. Now let's find the exact answer. To subtract $76\frac{1}{2} - 39\frac{5}{8}$, we begin by finding the LCD of $\frac{1}{2}$ and $\frac{5}{8}$. First we list multiples of 2 and 8:

$$2: \quad 2, 4, 6, \circledR, \ldots$$
$$8: \quad \circledR, 16, 24, \ldots$$

Since the smallest number in both lists is 8, the LCD of $\frac{1}{2}$ and $\frac{5}{8}$ is 8. Changing $\frac{1}{2}$ to an equivalent fraction with a denominator of 8, we obtain the following:

$$\frac{1}{2} = \frac{1 \times 4}{2 \times 4} = \frac{4}{8}$$

Therefore, $$76\frac{1}{2} - 39\frac{5}{8} = 76\frac{4}{8} - 39\frac{5}{8}$$

To subtract mixed numbers, we subtract the whole number and fractional parts separately. We cannot subtract the fractional parts because $\frac{4}{8} < \frac{5}{8}$. Therefore, we must rewrite the first fraction so that it has a larger numerator.

To do that, we subtract 1 from the whole number part of the mixed number $76\frac{4}{8}$ to get 75, and add 1 in the form of the fraction $\frac{8}{8}$ to the fractional part of $76\frac{4}{8}$ to get $\frac{12}{8}$. The resulting mixed number is $75\frac{12}{8}$, as shown here:

$$76\frac{1}{2} = 76\frac{4}{8} = 75 + 1 + \frac{4}{8} = 75 + \frac{8}{8} + \frac{4}{8} = 75\frac{12}{8}$$

We chose to rewrite 1 as the fraction $\frac{8}{8}$ because 8 is our LCD, making it easy to add to $\frac{4}{8}$. Since $\frac{12}{8} > \frac{5}{8}$, we can now solve the problem $75\frac{12}{8} - 39\frac{5}{8}$. It often helps to write problems involving addition and subtraction of fractions vertically, as follows:

$$76\frac{1}{2} = \quad 76\frac{1 \times 4}{2 \times 4} = \quad 76\frac{4}{8} = \quad 75 + 1 + \frac{4}{8} = \quad 75 + \frac{8}{8} + \frac{4}{8} = \quad 75\frac{12}{8}$$

$$-39\frac{5}{8} = -39\frac{5}{8} \qquad = -39\frac{5}{8} = -39\frac{5}{8} \qquad\qquad = -39\frac{5}{8} \qquad\qquad = -39\frac{5}{8}$$

$$36\frac{7}{8}$$

Subtract whole numbers: $75 - 39 = 36$.

Subtract fractional parts: $\frac{12}{8} - \frac{5}{8} = \frac{7}{8}$.

Therefore, there are $36\frac{7}{8}$ inches of space left along the wall for a filing cabinet. Since $36\frac{7}{8}$ is close to our estimate of 37 inches, this answer is reasonable.

FRACTIONS IN DAILY LIFE: MEASURING FABRIC

Let's consider another example. Suppose you have a bolt of $25\frac{1}{2}$ yards of linen to make tablecloths. If each tablecloth requires $2\frac{1}{8}$ yards of fabric, how many can be made from this bolt of linen? To determine the answer, you solve the following problem:

$$25\frac{1}{2} \div 2\frac{1}{8}$$

Before we begin, we will first estimate what would be an appropriate answer. Since $25\frac{1}{2} \approx 26$ and $2\frac{1}{8} \approx 2$ and $26 \div 2 = 13$, our final answer should be close to 13 tablecloths. Now let's solve the problem.

To divide mixed numbers, we first change each mixed number to an improper fraction. We then multiply the first fraction by the reciprocal of the second fraction. If possible, to simplify the problem before completing the multiplication, we divide the numerator and denominator by a series of common factors. We show this by crossing out or canceling each number as it is divided by each common factor. This procedure is illustrated here.

$$25\frac{1}{2} \div 2\frac{1}{8} = \frac{51}{2} \div \frac{17}{8}$$
    Change each mixed number to an improper fraction.

$$= \frac{51}{2} \cdot \frac{8}{17}$$
    Multiply $\frac{51}{2}$ by the reciprocal of $\frac{17}{8}$, which is $\frac{8}{17}$.

$$= \frac{51 \cdot 8}{2 \cdot 17}$$
    Multiply the numerators and denominators.

$$= \frac{51 \cdot \overset{4}{\cancel{8}}}{\underset{1}{\cancel{2}} \cdot 17}$$
    Divide both numerator and denominator by 2: $8 \div 2 = 4$. Cancel 8 and write 4 above it. $2 \div 2 = 1$. Cancel 2 and write 1 below it.

$$= \frac{\overset{3}{\cancel{51}} \cdot \overset{4}{\cancel{8}}}{\underset{1}{\cancel{2}} \cdot \underset{1}{\cancel{17}}}$$
    Divide numerator and denominator by 17: $51 \div 17 = 3$. Cancel 51 and write 3 above it. $17 \div 17 = 1$. Cancel 17 and write 1 below it.

$$= \frac{3 \cdot 4}{1 \cdot 1}$$
    Multiply the remaining numbers in the numerator and denominator.

$$= \frac{12}{1} = 12$$
    Simplify the result.

We can therefore make 12 tablecloths from the bolt of linen. Since 12 is close to our estimate of 13, this answer is reasonable.

STRATEGIES FOR SUCCESS

By now, you might be feeling overwhelmed by the amount of material we have just discussed dealing with fractions. You might feel that it will be a long time before you are able to easily solve a complicated problem from start to finish without panicking or making a careless mistake. However, many of the techniques we have discussed are building blocks for understanding other mathematical concepts that we will be discussing throughout the book. Don't get discouraged. Fractions are difficult. With time and practice, you will have greater confidence in your ability to understand fractions. Here is a summary of what you can do to help yourself "fight the fear of fractions."

STRATEGIES FOR SUCCESS WITH FRACTIONS

1. Learn the meaning of important terms.
2. Learn all the multiplication tables through 12.
3. Do lots of problems to build confidence and speed.
4. Write down a strategy for doing multistep problems.
5. Work slowly and carefully to avoid careless mistakes.

CHAPTER 4 EXERCISES

1. Describe two situations where you encountered fractions in your daily life during the past month.
2. Explain in your own words how you find the LCD of two fractions and why you might need to do so. Give an example that illustrates this procedure.
3. Find a recipe that includes fractional amounts. Calculate the amount of each ingredient you would use if you doubled the recipe.
4. What operations with fractions cause you the greatest difficulty? Plan a strategy to help you develop your skill in this area.

CHAPTER

Daring to Do Decimals

MATH MEMORIES

"I was sick when our class learned how to divide decimals in 6th grade, and every year I fell deeper into the hole of not knowing how to do math."

"All I remember about decimals is that you have to be careful to put the decimal point in the right place. I never knew where that place was, so I could never get the right answer."

"I am so bad at math that I can't even balance my checkbook. I just assume that the bank is right and hope that I don't overdraw my checking account."

"I avoid anything financial, economic, or mathematical. I rely on my husband to balance the checkbook and figure out the restaurant bills."

COMMON PROBLEMS

Decimals are probably among the most familiar numbers to you because you see them whenever you deal with money. However, when you are required to perform calculations on numbers with a large number of decimal places, you may become confused and frustrated. One reason many people have difficulty with decimals is that they tend to perform calculations on decimals in a very mechanical way, without any understanding of the value of a number written in decimal notation. People also tend to become frustrated when they make a lot of careless mistakes in adding, subtracting, multiplying, and dividing decimals. Many adults have trouble balancing their checkbooks, even if they use a calculator, because the more numbers they enter into the calculator, the more likely it is that they will hit the wrong key.

Division of decimals is particularly difficult because it is a multistep process, similar to that for division of whole numbers, and it is likely that many adults have forgotten the technique. Finally, decimals with lots of zeros may seem very intimidating. Since we do not usually work with very small or very large numbers in our daily lives, it is easy to forget how to perform operations on numbers with lots of zeros.

HINTS FOR STUDYING DECIMALS

When you begin to study decimals, take some time to learn how to read decimals properly. This will give you a clear understanding of the relationship between fractions and decimals, and it will help you to remember how to perform various operations on decimals. Also, when you study percents, you will have to convert percents to both fractions and decimals, and vice versa. If it is difficult for you to convert decimals to fractions and fractions to decimals, it will be difficult for you to work confidently with percents.

Addition, subtraction, and multiplication of decimals are relatively straightforward operations. However, you may often be frustrated when you try to rush through a problem and make careless mistakes. To catch obvious errors, it is helpful to estimate the answer before you perform the calculation. This is especially important when you are using a calculator.

Since the procedure for dividing decimals is similar to that for dividing whole numbers, it is very helpful to review the division of whole numbers. You should then supplement that knowledge with the specific techniques for dividing decimals. Be certain to work slowly and carefully. Dividing decimals requires many steps, and it is easy to make mistakes.

To be able to work confidently with decimals that have lots of zeros, it is helpful to think of simple examples to remind you of the techniques. It is sometimes useful to convert the decimals to fractions, perform the same operation by using the fractional equivalents, and then compare your answers using fractions to those answers obtained by using decimals.

NAMING DECIMALS

When a number is written in decimal notation, it is important that you learn how to read it correctly so that you can understand what the decimal represents. We know that the quantity $7.42 represents 7 dollars and 42 cents. Similarly, the decimal 7.42 should be read as "seven *and* forty-two hundredths." This makes sense because there are 100 cents in 1 dollar and 100 hundredths is equal to 1.

$$100 \times \frac{1}{100} = 1$$

When we read 7.42 as "seven point four two," it does not clearly indicate the value of the number.

We name decimals based on the location or place value of each digit in the number. The word *and* indicates the location of the decimal point. When a decimal is named correctly, it is easy to determine its fractional equivalent. For example, the decimal 7.42 (seven and forty-two hundredths) is equal to the mixed number $7\frac{42}{100}$. Here is a list of some decimals, in order of decreasing size, and their fractional equivalents:

$$0.3 = \frac{3}{10} \qquad\qquad \text{three tenths}$$

$$0.03 = \frac{3}{100} \qquad\qquad \text{three hundredths}$$

$$0.003 = \frac{3}{1,000} \qquad\qquad \text{three thousandths}$$

$$0.0003 = \frac{3}{10,000} \qquad\qquad \text{three ten-thousandths}$$

$$0.00003 = \frac{3}{100,000} \qquad\qquad \text{three hundred-thousandths}$$

$$0.000003 = \frac{3}{1,000,000} \qquad\qquad \text{three millionths}$$

The names of decimal places end in "ths" and follow the same pattern as the names of whole numbers. For example, the number 5,268,413.759264 is read as "five million, two hundred sixty-eight thousand, four hundred thirteen *and* seven hundred fifty-nine thousand, two hundred sixty-four millionths". The place value of each digit is shown in Figure 5.1.

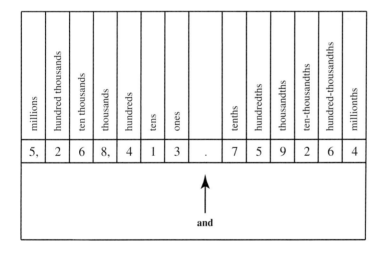

Figure 5.1

ESTIMATION

Many problems in doing arithmetic with decimals are caused by careless mistakes. One way to reduce mistakes is to mentally estimate the answers before doing the actual calculations. We can often catch errors by checking that the answers we obtain are close to our preliminary estimates.

To obtain an approximate value for a number, we use a process called *rounding off*. To indicate the accuracy of your approximation, state the place value to which you are rounding off. For example, if a bushel of apples weighs 21.836 pounds, you could also say that it weighs about 20 pounds. In fact, we can also approximate that weight in a variety of ways. The symbol ≈ means "approximately equal to."

$21.836 \approx 20$ rounded off to the nearest ten

$21.836 \approx 22$ rounded off to the nearest whole number

$21.836 \approx 21.8$ rounded off to the nearest tenth

$21.836 \approx 21.84$ rounded off to the nearest hundredth

When we round off to the nearest ten, we are saying that 21.836 is closer to 20 than to 30. When we round off to the nearest whole number, we are saying that 21.836 is closer to 22 than to 21. When we round off to the nearest tenth, we are saying that 21.836 is closer to 21.8 than to 21.9. When we round off to the nearest hundredth, we are saying that 21.836 is closer to 21.84 than to 21.83. Generally, the smaller the place value to which we are rounding off, the more accurate is the estimate. For example, 21.84 (nearest hundredth) is a more accurate approximation of the number 21.836 than 20 (nearest ten). This is illustrated in Figure 5.2.

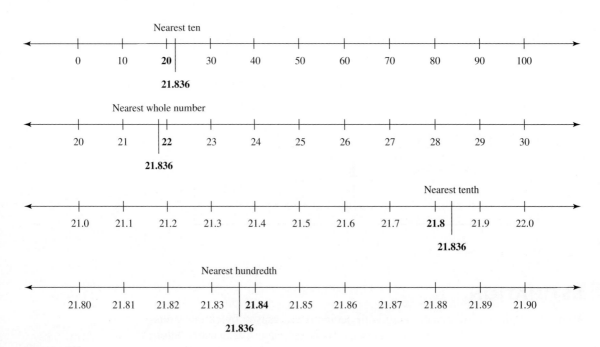

Figure 5.2

The procedure used to round off a number is summarized here:

To Round Off a Number

1. Examine the digit one place value to the right of the place value to which you are rounding off.
2. If it is greater than or equal to 5 (≥ 5), add 1 to the digit in the place value to which you are rounding off, and drop the digits to its right.
3. If it is less than 5 (< 5), keep the digit in the place value to which you are rounding off the same, and drop the digits to its right.

Consider these examples:

1. Round off 8,374 to the nearest hundred.

$$8,\underline{3}74$$

   The digit 3 is in the hundreds place. The digit 7 is on its right. Since $7 > 5$, we add 1 to the 3. Therefore,

$$8,\underline{3}74 \approx 8,400$$

2. Round off 4.639 to the nearest tenth.

$$4.\underline{6}39$$

   The digit 6 is in the tenths place. The digit 3 is on its right. Since $3 < 5$, we leave 6 as it is. Therefore,

$$4.\underline{6}39 \approx 4.6$$

3. Round off 27.51 to the nearest whole number.

$$2\underline{7}.51$$

   The digit 7 is in the ones place. The digit 5 is on its right. Since $5 \geq 5$, we add 1 to the 7. Therefore,

$$2\underline{7}.51 \approx 28$$

Now that you know the technique for rounding off numbers, you can use it to estimate your answers when adding, subtracting, multiplying, and dividing numbers. Performing these calculations with rounded-off numbers is easier because the calculations are simpler. Keep in mind, however, that the accuracy of your estimated answer depends on how close the rounded-off numbers are to the actual numbers.

ADDITION AND SUBTRACTION OF DECIMALS

We will now look at some common examples of how we use decimals in our daily lives. Addition and subtraction of decimals are the easiest operations to perform, but people still tend to make a lot of careless mistakes. One way to catch obvious errors is to round off the numbers being added or subtracted and estimate your answer, before you perform the actual calculation.

Consider the following example. At the beginning of the month your checking account had a balance of $528.13. During the month you wrote checks for $37.29, $84.56, $613.50, $492.28, and $41.07. You also made deposits of $803.44 and $74.98. What is your balance at the end of the month? To solve the problem, first add the two deposits to the balance at the beginning of the month. From that value, you can subtract the total amount of all the checks written during the month, to find the ending balance.

Before you perform the actual calculation, estimate the answer by rounding off each number to the nearest ten dollars. First estimate the sum of the beginning balance and the two deposits:

$$\$528.13 \approx \$\ \ 530$$
$$803.44 \approx \ \ \ \ 800$$
$$74.98 \approx \ \ \ \ \underline{70}$$
$$\$1,400$$

Next, estimate the total of all the checks written during the month:

$$\$\ 37.29 \approx \$\ \ \ \ 40$$
$$84.56 \approx \ \ \ \ 80$$
$$613.50 \approx \ \ \ \ 610$$
$$492.28 \approx \ \ \ \ 490$$
$$41.07 \approx \ \ \ \ \underline{40}$$
$$\$1,260$$

Finally, estimate the ending balance by finding the difference between the two estimates:

$$\$1,400$$
$$\underline{-\ 1,260}$$
$$\$\ \ 140$$

Therefore, the estimated ending balance is $140.

Now let's calculate the actual answer. When you add the deposits to the beginning balance, write the numbers vertically, lining up the decimal points. Then add the numbers in each column, moving from right to left. If the sum of the digits in any column is greater than 9, carry the value of the number in the tens place to the next column. The decimal point should be placed in the answer directly under the column of decimal points in the numbers being added:

$$
\begin{array}{r}
{\scriptstyle 1\,1\,1\ \ 1} \\
\$\ \ 528.13 \\
803.44 \\
\underline{74.98} \\
\$1,406.55
\end{array}
$$

Now use the same procedure to find the sum of the checks written during the month:

$$
\begin{array}{r}
{\scriptstyle 2\,1\,1\ \ 3} \\
\$\ \ \ 37.29 \\
84.56 \\
613.50 \\
492.28 \\
\underline{41.07} \\
\$1,268.70
\end{array}
$$

To find the balance at the end of the month, subtract the sum of the checks from the sum of the beginning balance and deposits. First, write the numbers, vertically lining up the decimal points. Subtract the numbers in each column, moving from right to left. If a digit in the top number is less than the bottom digit in the same column, subtract (borrow) 1 from the digit to its left and add 10 to that digit. If the digit you need to subtract 1 from is a 0, subtract 1 from the digit to its left, and add 10 to the 0 to get 10. Then subtract 1 from the 10 to get 9, and add 10 to the original digit. Be sure to place a decimal point in the answer directly under the column of decimal points in the numbers being subtracted:

$$
\begin{array}{r}
\$1,406.55 \\
-\,1,268.70 \\
\end{array}
\qquad
\begin{array}{r}
{\scriptstyle 3\ \ 9\ 15} \\
\$1,4^{1}\not0\not6.^{1}55 \\
-\,1,2\ 6\,8.\ 70 \\
\hline
\$\ \ 1\ 3\,7.\ 85
\end{array}
$$

The closing balance at the end of the month is $137.85. Since this is close to our estimated answer of $140, this answer is reasonable.

The procedures for adding and subtracting decimals are summarized here:

To Add Decimals

1. Write the numbers to be added in a column, lining up the decimal points.
2. Add the digits in each column, moving from right to left.
3. If the sum of the digits in any column exceeds 9, carry the digit in the tens place of the sum to the next column.
4. Place a decimal point in the answer, directly under the column of decimal points in the numbers being added.

To Subtract Decimals

1. Write the numbers to be subtracted in a column, lining up the decimal points.
2. Subtract the digits in each column, moving from right to left.
3. If a digit in the top number is less than the bottom digit in the same column, borrow 1 from the digit to its left and add 10 to that digit.

4. Place a decimal point in the answer, directly under the column of decimal points in the numbers being subtracted.

Remember that, as is the case with subtracting whole numbers, if the digit you need to subtract 1 from is a 0, subtract 1 from the digit to its left, and add 10 to the 0 to get 10. Then subtract 1 from the 10 to get 9, and add 10 to the original digit.

MULTIPLICATION OF DECIMALS

Problems that require the multiplication of decimals can cause difficulty for two reasons. You may be intimidated by numbers that include lots of zeros, or you may rush through a calculation too quickly and make careless mistakes. This section discusses methods for overcoming both of these obstacles.

In learning the technique for multiplying decimals, it is helpful to look at the results obtained by multiplying their fractional equivalents. Several examples are given here.

$$0.7 \times 0.4 = \frac{7}{10} \times \frac{4}{10} = \frac{28}{100} = 0.28 \qquad \text{2 decimal places}$$

$$0.7 \times 0.04 = \frac{7}{10} \times \frac{4}{100} = \frac{28}{1,000} = 0.028 \qquad \text{3 decimal places}$$

$$0.7 \times 0.004 = \frac{7}{10} \times \frac{4}{1,000} = \frac{28}{10,000} = 0.0028 \qquad \text{4 decimal places}$$

$$0.07 \times 0.004 = \frac{7}{100} \times \frac{4}{1,000} = \frac{28}{100,000} = 0.00028 \qquad \text{5 decimal places}$$

$$0.007 \times 0.004 = \frac{7}{1,000} \times \frac{4}{1,000} = \frac{28}{1,000,000} = 0.000028 \qquad \text{6 decimal places}$$

Notice that in each case, the number of decimal places in the answer is equal to the sum of the number of decimal places in the numbers being multiplied. We can therefore use the following technique for multiplying decimals.

To Multiply Decimals

1. Multiply the numbers, ignoring the decimal points.

2. Place a decimal point in the answer so that the number of decimal places in the product equals the sum of the number of decimal places in the factors.

For example,

$$0.2 \quad \times \quad 0.3 \quad = \quad 0.06$$
$$\uparrow \qquad\qquad \uparrow \qquad\qquad \uparrow$$

1 decimal place $+$ 1 decimal place $=$ 2 decimal places

$$0.5 \quad \times \quad 0.04 \quad = \quad 0.020$$
$$\uparrow \qquad\qquad \uparrow \qquad\qquad \uparrow$$

1 decimal place $+$ 2 decimal places $=$ 3 decimal places

$$0.08 \quad \times \quad 0.06 \quad = \quad 0.0048$$
$$\uparrow \qquad\qquad \uparrow \qquad\qquad \uparrow$$

2 decimal places $+$ 2 decimal places $=$ 4 decimal places

If you forget the technique for multiplying decimals, change each decimal to a fraction, multiply the fractions, and change the result to a decimal.

DECIMALS IN DAILY LIFE: CALCULATING COST

Let us now solve the following problem. If hazelnut coffee costs $4.29 per pound, how much does 1.75 pounds of hazelnut coffee cost? To solve this problem, multiply $4.29 by 1.75. Before we do the actual multiplication, let us estimate the answer.

$$
\begin{array}{r}
\$4.29 \approx \$4 \\
\underline{\times\ 1.75 \approx\ 2} \\
\$8 \quad \text{the estimate}
\end{array}
$$

Now let us determine the exact answer.

$$
\begin{array}{r}
{\scriptstyle 2\ 6} \\
{\scriptstyle 1\ 4} \\
\$\ 4.29 \quad \text{2 decimal places} \\
\underline{\times\ 1.75} \quad \text{2 decimal places} \\
2145 \\
3003 \\
\underline{429} \\
\$7.5075 \quad \text{4 decimal places}
\end{array}
$$

Since the answer expresses an amount of money, we round off $7.5075 to the nearest cent, to obtain $7.51. The coffee therefore costs $7.51, which is a reasonable answer since it is close to our estimate of $8.

Since multiplication of decimals can be very time-consuming, it is usually done with a pocket calculator. We should always estimate our answers before using a calculator, because it is easy to make a mistake by pressing the wrong button, especially with numbers that have lots of digits.

DIVISION OF DECIMALS

Dividing decimals is probably one of the most difficult and time-consuming calculations in arithmetic. The procedure for dividing decimals requires combining our understanding of the notion of place value with the technique for dividing whole numbers. Since we often use a pocket calculator to divide decimals, it is also important that we learn to obtain accurate estimates of our answers before we perform the division.

When we divide decimals, we rewrite the problem so that the divisor is a whole number. This can be achieved by multiplying both the dividend and the divisor by a multiple of 10. This process can be illustrated by rewriting the division problem as a fraction. For example,

$$42 \div 0.7 = \frac{42}{0.7} = \frac{42 \times 10}{0.7 \times 10} = \frac{420}{7} = 60$$

$$42 \div 0.07 = \frac{42}{0.07} = \frac{42 \times 100}{0.07 \times 100} = \frac{4{,}200}{7} = 600$$

$$42 \div 0.007 = \frac{42}{0.007} = \frac{42 \times 1{,}000}{0.007 \times 1{,}000} = \frac{42{,}000}{7} = 6{,}000$$

This process can be simplified by moving the decimal point the same number of places to the right in the dividend and in the divisor. For example, when we solved the problem $42 \div 0.07$, we multiplied both numerator and denominator by 100, which is the same as moving the decimal point 2 places to the right in the dividend and in the divisor.

$$42 \div 0.07 = \frac{42.}{0.07} = \frac{42.00}{0.07} = \frac{4{,}200}{7} = 600$$

Notice that we had to attach two 0s to the number in the numerator in order to move the decimal point two places to the right. Using standard division notation, we can rewrite this problem as follows:

$$0.07\overline{)42.00} = 6\,00$$

Instead of using arrows, we often use a symbol called a *caret* ($\wedge$) to show the new location of the decimal point:

$$0.07_{\wedge} \overline{\smash{)}42.00_{\wedge}} \atop 6\,00$$

The procedure for dividing decimals can be summarized as follows.

To Divide Decimals

1. If the divisor is not a whole number, move the decimal point in the divisor and in the dividend to make the divisor a whole number. Use a caret ($\wedge$) to indicate the new location of the decimal point.

2. Place a decimal point in the quotient immediately above its new location in the dividend.

3. Divide the two numbers, using the technique for dividing whole numbers.

DECIMALS IN DAILY LIFE: CALCULATING MILEAGE

Let us now use this technique to solve the following problem. If a car traveled 61.74 miles on 2.1 gallons of gas, how many miles per gallon did the car get on that trip? To solve this problem, we divide 61.74 by 2.1. Before we do that, we first estimate the answer:

$$61.74 \text{ miles} \div 2.1 \text{ gallons} \approx 60 \text{ miles} \div 2 \text{ gallons} = \frac{60 \text{ miles}}{2 \text{ gallons}} = 30 \text{ miles/gallon}$$

Our estimate is 30 miles/gallon, or 30 miles per gallon. Now we will determine the exact answer for 61.74 miles ÷ 2.1 gallons.

$$
\begin{array}{r}
2\,9.4 \\
2.1_{\wedge}\overline{\smash{)}61.7_{\wedge}4} \\
-42 \\
\hline
19\,7 \\
-18\,9 \\
\hline
8\,4 \\
-8\,4 \\
\hline
0
\end{array}
$$

1. Move the decimal point 1 place to the right in the dividend and divisor.
2. 21 goes into 61 about 2 times. Put 2 over the 1 in the dividend.
   21 × 2 = 42. 61 − 42 = 19. Bring down the 7 from the dividend.
3. 21 goes into 197 about 9 times. Put 9 over the 7 in the dividend.
   21 × 9 = 189. 197 − 189 = 8. Bring down the 4 from the dividend.
4. 21 goes into 84 four times. Put 4 over the 4 in the dividend.
   21 × 4 = 84. 84 − 84 = 0.

Therefore, the car got 29.4 miles per gallon on the trip. This answer is reasonable since it is close to our estimate of 30 miles per gallon.

STRATEGIES FOR SUCCESS

At this point, you may feel a bit more familiar with decimals and have a better understanding of the notion of place value. Even though addition and subtraction of decimals may seem relatively straightforward, multiplication and division are much more difficult, especially when the numbers have many digits. In many situations, you will probably use a calculator to do the more difficult problems. However, the importance of first estimating your answers cannot be overstated. If you are able to accurately approximate your answers whenever you use a calculator, you will have acquired a useful skill for finding the most obvious errors. Here is a summary of the strategies we have discussed in this chapter to encourage you in "daring to do decimals."

STRATEGIES FOR SUCCESS WITH DECIMALS

1. Learn the names of place values and use them to name decimals.

2. Work slowly and carefully and estimate your answers.

3. Review the technique for dividing whole numbers.

4. Become proficient in doing operations on decimals with lots of zeros.

 CHAPTER 5 EXERCISES

1. Balance your checkbook when your next bank statement comes in the mail. What steps did you take to minimize careless mistakes?

2. The next time you go to the store, estimate the total cost of your purchases before the cashier shows you the total. How close was your estimate?

3. Find out the typical annual salary for someone in a profession you may want to enter. Estimate the monthly gross salary and then determine the exact answer.

CHAPTER

6

Gaining Proficiency with Percents

MATH MEMORIES

"Not knowing math affects me all the time. I avoid counting the change when I buy something. I need someone else to figure out the tip when I go to a restaurant. I even avoid going to stores advertising sales because I can't figure out percents."

"It's frustrating to realize that percents exist everywhere in the real world and I usually don't have a clue as to what they mean."

"I went to a job interview and the employer asked me, 'What is 20% of 120?' I couldn't answer the question, so I didn't get the job."

"I have a hard time doing budgets at work, so I use a calculator to do percents since I have no idea how to figure them out on my own. In hindsight, had I not been so petrified of math, I would have majored in business instead of psychology."

"If I had really learned math in school, I might have been an architect, or a physicist, or just a regular person who can understand percents and know what my mutual funds are really earning."

COMMON PROBLEMS

Percents are one of the most common mathematical quantities we encounter in daily life. It seems as if every time we open a newspaper or turn on the TV, we see a percent being used to illustrate a point. An economic report might announce that the prime interest rate fell to $2\frac{1}{4}\%$ or that the unemployment rate rose to $6\frac{1}{2}\%$. The weather forecast might predict a 30% chance of rain or state that the relative humidity is 72%. Your boss might tell you that you will be getting a 7% raise, and when you go to a restaurant to celebrate, you need to leave a 15% tip. Since we are constantly confronted with situations that require us to use percents, it is not surprising that we feel anxious or embarrassed when we cannot figure out exactly what quantity is represented by a percent.

One reason why percents seem so confusing is that we do not have a firm understanding of fractions and decimals. The same quantity can often be represented by using a fraction, a decimal, or a percent. In some situations, one form for a number will make more sense to us than another. For example, we might say that $\frac{1}{4}$ of a pie was left uneaten, or that a toll costs \$0.25, or that 25% of the people in a room are wearing glasses. Even though $\frac{1}{4} = 0.25 = 25\%$, these different representations for the same quantity are not always used interchangeably. To fully understand the meaning of a percent, it is necessary to learn the relationship between fractions, decimals, and percents, and to be able to convert numbers from one form to another.

Another problem is that we do not fully understand what quantity is represented by a percent. We might recall that 50% is the same as $\frac{1}{2}$, or that 25% is the same as $\frac{1}{4}$, but since we do not know the procedure for converting a percent to a fraction, we cannot determine what is meant by 2% or 200%.

Percents that include fractional and decimal parts are especially confusing to people. If we do not know what quantity is represented by 30%, it is even harder to determine what is meant by $33\frac{1}{3}\%$ or 27.85%.

Many people find percents difficult because they cannot remember how to convert between decimals and percents. They do not know in which direction to move the decimal point, and they are unable to figure it out because they lack a real understanding of the relationship between fractions and decimals.

Word problems involving percents intimidate many people, especially those involving percent increase and percent decrease. Since many applications in daily life, such as determining your new salary when you get a raise or finding the sale price when an item is marked down, involve percent increase and decrease, it is important to be able to master this concept.

HINTS FOR STUDYING PERCENTS

To gain a thorough understanding of percents, it is best to begin by reviewing your knowledge of fractions and decimals. Once you are able to convert between fractions and decimals without difficulty, it will be easier for you to learn the techniques for converting between percents and fractions and between percents and decimals. Do not simply memorize the procedures for converting between fractions, decimals, and percents. Always keep in mind *why* a mathematical technique works, and if you ever forget a technique, think of a simple example.

Always keep in mind the definition of a percent. The word ***percent*** means "per 100" or "parts of 100." Therefore, 50% means 50 parts of 100, or $\frac{50}{100}$, which reduces to $\frac{1}{2}$. If we state that 50% of the people at a conference are women, we mean that one-half of the people are women. Likewise, 100% means 100 parts of 100, or $\frac{100}{100}$, which is equal to 1. The statement $100\% = 1$ may seem confusing to you since we think of 100% as a large quantity and 1 as a small quantity. However, it is consistent with the definition of a percent and the fact that $50\% = \frac{1}{2}$. Consider this example. If you get 100% on a test, you answered every question correctly. In other words, you completed one whole test without an error. If you received a score of 50%, you answered only one-half of the questions on the test correctly.

When you are working with percents, it is helpful to remember the fractional and decimal equivalents of common percents. When you see percents with decimal and fractional parts, determine an approximation that is equivalent to a percent that is familiar to you. For example, if the quantity 24.62% confuses you, think of it as being approximately equal to 25%. Learning how to approximate the value of percents and to estimate your answers to problems that involve percents will also help you determine if your answers are reasonable and avoid obvious mistakes.

To gain confidence in solving word problems that involve percents, you need to become familiar with a wide variety of applications and work through many examples of each type of problem. Since applications involving percent increase and percent decrease can be especially difficult, it may help to work out a similar problem with simple numbers first, to help you to understand the needed mathematical procedures. Before you complete a problem, be sure to round off the numbers involved in the calculation and estimate your answer, so you can catch obvious errors.

CONVERTING PERCENTS TO FRACTIONS

We will now discuss the techniques for converting between fractions, decimals, and percents. To convert a number from a percent to a fraction, we use the definition of a percent. Recall that percent means "per 100" or parts of 100. Therefore, we can rewrite a percent as a fraction with a denominator of 100. If necessary, we can reduce the fraction to lowest terms. Consider these examples, illustrated in Figure 6.1.

$$25\% = \frac{25}{100} = \frac{1}{4}$$

$$50\% = \frac{50}{100} = \frac{1}{2}$$

$$75\% = \frac{75}{100} = \frac{3}{4}$$

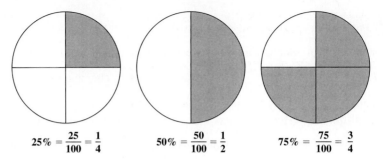

$$25\% = \frac{25}{100} = \frac{1}{4} \qquad 50\% = \frac{50}{100} = \frac{1}{2} \qquad 75\% = \frac{75}{100} = \frac{3}{4}$$

Figure 6.1

The fractional equivalents of other common percents are illustrated in Figure 6.2.

$$20\% = \frac{20}{100} = \frac{1}{5}$$

$$40\% = \frac{40}{100} = \frac{2}{5}$$

$$60\% = \frac{60}{100} = \frac{3}{5}$$

$$80\% = \frac{80}{100} = \frac{4}{5}$$

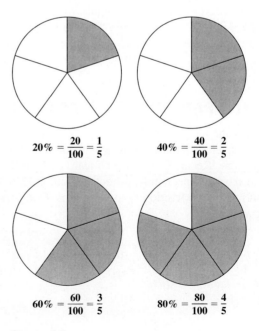

$$20\% = \frac{20}{100} = \frac{1}{5} \qquad 40\% = \frac{40}{100} = \frac{2}{5}$$

$$60\% = \frac{60}{100} = \frac{3}{5} \qquad 80\% = \frac{80}{100} = \frac{4}{5}$$

Figure 6.2

Percents that are equivalent to numbers greater than 1 can be converted to mixed numbers in a similar fashion. See Figure 6.3.

$$125\% = \frac{125}{100} = \frac{5}{4} = 1\frac{1}{4}$$

$$150\% = \frac{150}{100} = \frac{3}{2} = 1\frac{1}{2}$$

$$275\% = \frac{275}{100} = \frac{11}{4} = 2\frac{3}{4}$$

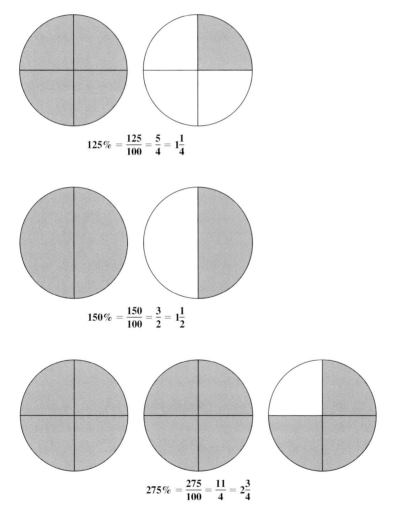

$$125\% = \frac{125}{100} = \frac{5}{4} = 1\frac{1}{4}$$

$$150\% = \frac{150}{100} = \frac{3}{2} = 1\frac{1}{2}$$

$$275\% = \frac{275}{100} = \frac{11}{4} = 2\frac{3}{4}$$

Figure 6.3

The procedure for converting a percent to a fraction is summarized here:

To Convert a Percent to a Fraction

1. Rewrite the percent as a fraction with a denominator of 100.

2. Reduce the fraction to lowest terms.

The technique for converting a fractional percent such as $\frac{1}{5}\%$ or $33\frac{1}{3}\%$ to a fraction is a bit more complicated. When you rewrite the percent as a fraction having a denominator of 100, you are left with a complex fraction that has either a fraction or a mixed number in the numerator. If the numerator is a mixed number, you rewrite it as an improper fraction. You then multiply the numerator and denominator by the denominator of the fraction in the numerator, to make the numerator a whole number. Finally, if necessary, you reduce the resulting fraction to lowest terms. We can now use this procedure to convert a common fractional percent, $33\frac{1}{3}\%$, to a fraction.

$$33\frac{1}{3}\% = \frac{33\frac{1}{3}}{100}$$ Rewrite the percent as a fraction with a denominator of 100.

$$= \frac{\frac{100}{3}}{100}$$ Rewrite the numerator as an improper fraction.

$$= \frac{\frac{100}{3} \times 3}{100 \times 3}$$ Multiply the numerator and the denominator by 3 to eliminate the fraction in the numerator.

$$= \frac{100}{300}$$

$$= \frac{1}{3}$$ Reduce to lowest terms.

Another common fractional percent, $66\frac{2}{3}\%$, represents twice the value of $33\frac{1}{3}\%$. The same technique can be used to show that $66\frac{2}{3}\%$ is equal to $\frac{2}{3}$. See Figure 6.4.

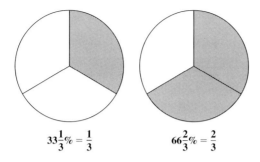

$$33\frac{1}{3}\% = \frac{1}{3} \qquad\qquad 66\frac{2}{3}\% = \frac{2}{3}$$

Figure 6.4

A percent containing a decimal may be converted to a fraction in a similar way. For example, we can convert 2.5% to a fraction as follows:

$2.5\% = \dfrac{2.5}{100}$ Rewrite the percent as a fraction with a denominator of 100.

$= \dfrac{2.5 \times \mathbf{10}}{100 \times \mathbf{10}}$ Multiply both numerator and denominator by 10 to eliminate the decimal in the numerator.

$= \dfrac{25}{1,000}$

$= \dfrac{1}{40}$ Reduce to lowest terms.

CONVERTING PERCENTS TO DECIMALS

To illustrate the technique for converting a percent to a decimal, we can rewrite the percent as a fraction with a denominator of 100 and then convert that fraction to a decimal. Consider these examples:

$$70\% = \frac{70}{100} = 0.7$$

$$7\% = \frac{7}{100} = 0.07$$

$$0.7\% = \frac{0.7}{100} = \frac{0.7 \times \mathbf{10}}{100 \times \mathbf{10}} = \frac{7}{1,000} = 0.007$$

$$0.07\% = \frac{0.07}{100} = \frac{0.07 \times \mathbf{100}}{100 \times \mathbf{100}} = \frac{7}{10,000} = 0.0007$$

Notice that in each case, we obtain the same result by removing the percent sign and moving the decimal point two places to the left. We can therefore summarize the technique for converting a percent to a decimal as follows:

To Convert a Percent to a Decimal

1. Remove the percent sign.   2. Move the decimal point two places to the left.

We will now use this procedure to convert the following percents to decimals:

$36\% = \ 36. = 0.36$ Remove the percent sign. Move decimal
                                     point 2 places to left.

$8.29\% = \ 8.29 = 0.0829$ Remove the percent sign. Move decimal
                                     point 2 places to left.

$104.5\% = 104.5 = 1.045$ Remove the percent sign. Move decimal
                                     point 2 places to left.

If you ever forget this technique, you can always rewrite the percent as a fraction with a denominator of 100 (using the definition of a percent) and then convert that fraction to a decimal. It also helps to remember a simple example such as $25\% = 0.25$, which makes intuitive sense to us since 25% is also equal to $\frac{1}{4}$.

CONVERTING DECIMALS TO PERCENTS

To illustrate the technique for converting a decimal to a percent, we can rewrite the decimal as a fraction with a denominator of 100 and then rewrite that fraction as a percent, using the definition of a percent. Consider these examples:

$$0.75 = \frac{75}{100} = 75\%$$

$$0.03 = \frac{3}{100} = 3\%$$

$$0.864 = \frac{864}{1,000} = \frac{864 \div 10}{1,000 \div 10} = \frac{86.4}{100} = 86.4\%$$

$$1.92 = \frac{192}{100} = 192\%$$

Notice that in each case, we can obtain the same result by moving the decimal point two places to the right and attaching a percent sign. We can summarize the procedure for converting a decimal to a percent as follows:

To Convert a Decimal to a Percent

1. Move the decimal point two places to the right.   **2.** Attach a percent sign.

The following examples illustrate this technique:

$0.87 = 0.87 = 87\%$ Move decimal point 2 places to right.
Attach percent sign.

$0.0059 = 0.0059 = 0.59\%$ Move decimal point 2 places to right.
Attach percent sign.

$74.06 = 74.06 = 7,406\%$ Move decimal point 2 places to right.
Attach percent sign.

If you ever forget in which direction to move the decimal point when converting decimals to percents or percents to decimals, think of a common percent, such as 50%. We know that 50% is the same as one-half, or $50\% = 0.50$. We can see that to convert from a percent to a decimal, we move the decimal point two places to the **left,** and to convert from a decimal to a percent, we move the decimal point two places to the **right.**

CONVERTING FRACTIONS TO PERCENTS

To convert a fraction to a percent, we first convert the fraction to a decimal and then convert the decimal to a percent. For example, we can convert $\frac{3}{8}$ to a percent as follows:

$\frac{3}{8} = 3 \div 8$ 1. To convert $\frac{3}{8}$ to a decimal, divide $3 \div 8$.

$$
\begin{array}{r}
0.375 \\
8{\overline{\smash{\big)}\,3.000}} \\
\underline{-2\,4} \\
60 \\
\underline{-56} \\
40 \\
\underline{-40} \\
0
\end{array}
$$

$\frac{3}{8} = 0.375 = 37.5\%$ 2. To convert 0.375 to a percent, move decimal point 2 places to right and attach a percent sign.

The procedure for converting a fraction to a percent is summarized here.

To Convert a Fraction to a Percent

1. Convert the fraction to a decimal by dividing the numerator by the denominator.

2. Convert the decimal to a percent by moving the decimal point two places to the right and attaching a percent sign.

PERCENTS IN DAILY LIFE: DISCOUNTS

One of the most common examples of percents involves working with discounts. Consider this example. A store advertises that a suit is on sale for 20% off its original price. If the suit normally sells for $250, what is its sale price? One way to solve this problem is to first calculate the amount of the discount and then subtract the discount amount from the original price. We can summarize these steps with the following formulas:

$$\text{Discount Amount} = \text{Discount Rate} \times \text{Original Price}$$

$$\text{Sale Price} = \text{Original Price} - \text{Discount Amount}$$

In this problem, the discount rate is 20%, and the original price is $250. Therefore,

$$
\begin{aligned}
\text{Discount Amount} &= 20\% \times 250 && \\
&= 0.20 \times 250 && \text{Convert 20\% to a decimal.} \\
&= 50 && \text{Multiply.} \\
\text{Sale Price} &= 250 - 50 && \\
&= 200 && \text{Subtract.}
\end{aligned}
$$

The sale price is $200.

PERCENTS IN DAILY LIFE: INTEREST

Interest is the amount you earn for giving someone the use of your money, such as when you deposit money in a bank account, or the amount you pay to borrow money. The amount you deposit or borrow is called the **principal.** The longer you keep your money in the bank, the more interest you earn. The longer the term of a loan, the more interest you pay. To calculate the amount of interest on a given amount, we need to know both the rate at which interest is paid and the length of time the money is invested or borrowed. The interest rate is usually expressed as an annual percentage rate, that is, a percent that can be used to calculate the interest for a period of 1 year. To calculate the interest on an investment or loan for 1 year, we simply multiply the amount invested or borrowed (principal) by the interest rate. For 2 years, we would double that amount, for 3 years we would triple that amount, and so on. Therefore, to calculate the interest on a given amount of money, for a specific time period, we multiply the interest rate by the principal by the time. This is represented by the following formula for simple interest:

$$\text{Interest} = \text{Rate} \times \text{Principal} \times \text{Time}$$

Interest is the amount of interest, rate is the annual interest rate as a percent, principal is the amount invested or borrowed, and time is the number of years.

This is called the *simple interest formula* because it does not take into consideration the compounding of interest. Nowadays, interest is often compounded, or calculated multiple times during the year, so that interest is added to the principal and you start earning or paying interest on interest as the year progresses. Banks will sometimes advertise that interest on a certificate of deposit (CD) is compounded monthly. Thus at the end every month, the interest amount is calculated on the existing principal and is then added to that amount. Each month you earn larger amounts of interest since it is calculated using a larger principal. This calculation is now usually done by using computers, but the simple interest formula is still very useful because it gives us a very close approximation of the actual interest amount.

As an example, suppose you deposit $5,000 in a 3-year CD that pays an annual interest rate of 2%. How much interest will you have earned when the CD matures? In this example, the principal is $5,000, the interest rate is 2%, and the time is 3 years. We can use the simple interest formula to calculate the interest as follows:

$$
\begin{aligned}
\text{Interest} &= \text{Rate} \times \text{Principal} \times \text{Time} \\
&= 2\% \times \$5,000 \times 3 \\
&= 0.02 \times \$5,000 \times 3 \\
&= \$100 \times 3 \\
&= \$300
\end{aligned}
$$

Therefore, you will earn $300 in interest after 3 years, assuming no compounding of interest.

PERCENTS IN DAILY LIFE: TIPPING

Another common example of percents is seen in determining a tip. Consider this example. A restaurant bill for three people is $78.34. If the bill is to be divided equally, how much should each person leave the waiter if the diner would like to include a 15% tip? To solve this problem, we first need to calculate the amount of the tip, which is 15% of $78.34. We then need to add the tip amount to the bill amount. Finally, we divide the total amount by 3.

Before we solve this problem by using the exact numbers, it is a good idea to estimate the answer, so that we will be able to catch any obvious errors in the calculations. One way to estimate the tip amount is to regard the $78.34 bill as approximately equal to $80. We can mentally calculate that 10% of 80 is 8, and 5% of 80 is one-half of 8, or 4. Therefore, 15% of 80 is 8 + 4, or 12. We can then add the estimated tip amount of $12 to the approximate bill of $80 to obtain a total of $92. Since 92 is about equal to 93, and 93 divided by 3 is 31, each person should leave $31.

Let us now solve this problem by using the exact numbers.

$$\text{Tip Amount} = 15\% \text{ of } \$78.34$$
$$= 0.15 \times 78.34 \qquad \text{Multiply.}$$
$$= 11.7510$$
$$= \$11.75 \qquad \text{Round off to the nearest cent.}$$

$$\text{Total Amount} = \text{Bill Amount} + \text{Tip Amount}$$
$$= \$78.34 + \$11.75$$
$$= \$90.09$$

$$\text{Amount per Person} = \$90.09 \div 3$$
$$= \$30.03$$

Since $30.03 is close to our estimated answer of $31, this answer seems reasonable. In fact, since it is usually possible to mentally estimate the amount to pay in a restaurant, and many people do not like to do math in public places, it is very important to become confident in using this approximation technique. Since I usually prefer to overtip rather than undertip, I make sure that my approximations are a bit higher than the exact results.

PERCENTS IN DAILY LIFE: TAXES

Another common example of using percents involves taxes. Consider this example. If a pair of shoes sells for $40.00 and sales tax is $5\frac{1}{4}\%$, how much will it cost to purchase the shoes? To solve this problem, we need to calculate the tax amount and then add it to the price of the shoes to determine the total cost. Since $5\frac{1}{4}\% \approx 5\%$, we can estimate the answer as follows.

$$\text{Tax Amount} \approx 5\% \text{ of } \$40 = \$2 \qquad \text{Since } 10\% \text{ of } 40 \text{ is } 4$$
$$\text{Total Cost} = \text{Price} + \text{Tax Amount}$$
$$\approx \$40 + \$2 = \$42$$

The estimated cost is $42. Let us now determine the exact answer.

Tax Amount $= 5\frac{1}{4}\%$ of 40

$$= \frac{5\frac{1}{4}}{100} \times 40$$

1. Place $5\frac{1}{4}$ over a denominator of 100 to convert the percent to a fraction.

$$= 5\frac{1}{4} \div 100 \times 40$$

2. Rewrite the fraction as a division problem.

$$= \frac{21}{4} \times \frac{1}{100} \times \frac{40}{1}$$

3. Change $5\frac{1}{4}$ and 40 to improper fractions. To divide by 100, multiply by its reciprocal, $\frac{1}{100}$.

$$= \frac{21 \times 1 \times 40}{4 \times 100}$$

$$= \frac{21 \times 1 \times \overset{\overset{1}{\cancel{10}}}{\cancel{40}}}{\underset{1}{\cancel{4}} \times \underset{10}{\cancel{100}}}$$

4. Divide numerator and denominator by 4 and then by 10.

$$= \frac{21}{10}$$

$$= 2.1$$

Tax Amount $= \$2.10$

$$\text{Total Cost} = \text{Price} + \text{Tax Amount}$$
$$= \$40.00 + \$2.10$$
$$= \$42.10$$

The fact that the estimated cost of $42 is very close to the actual cost of $42.10 illustrates how useful it is to estimate answers when you are solving percent problems.

 # STRATEGIES FOR SUCCESS

Now that you have seen a number of practical examples, you probably have a better appreciation of why it is important to be able to convert between fractions, decimals, and percents. Even though percents may seem confusing at first, knowing the fractional equivalents of common percents, such as $33\frac{1}{3}\% = \frac{1}{3}$, will give you greater confidence in working with all types of percents, including those that include fractions. Remembering simple facts such as 75% = 0.75 will help you remember in which direction to move the decimal point when converting between decimals and percents. Finally, the importance of being able to first estimate your answers when solving percent problems cannot be overstated. Approximation is an extremely powerful tool that is especially useful in daily living situations when there is no need to calculate the exact answer because an estimate is close enough for all practical purposes. Here is a summary of the strategies for gaining proficiency with percents.

STRATEGIES FOR SUCCESS WITH PERCENTS

1. Learn the relationships between fractions, decimals, and percents.
2. Remember the fractional equivalents for common percents including percents that contain fractions.
3. Think of the decimal equivalent for a common percent to help you remember in which direction to move the decimal point when converting between decimals and percents.
4. Estimate your answers when solving problems with percents.

CHAPTER 6 EXERCISES

1. The next time you purchase something on sale, make note of the discount and estimate the sale price.
2. Look at your recent credit card statement, and determine the annual interest rate on the money borrowed while using that credit card. Calculate how much interest you would have to pay on your current balance after 2 years.
3. When you go out to a restaurant, estimate how much each person should pay, including tax and tip, if the bill is to be split equally.
4. Estimate the total cost of a purchase including the sales tax.
5. Look at an old income tax return, and try to determine how the final tax amount was computed.

C H A P T E R

Getting the Most out of Graphs

MATH MEMORIES

"Whenever I read a business article in the newspaper, I just skip over the graphs because they don't make sense to me."

"I have always wanted a career in business, but all those graphs and charts are just a blur to me."

"Because I am not a good math student, I have not been that successful in my business and health science courses. I need to learn how to interpret graphs and charts. As a tutor once said to me, being able to do math is just as important as being able to read."

COMMON PROBLEMS

Quite frequently, when we browse the Internet, look at a magazine, read the newspaper, or even watch a television news broadcast, we see that information is presented to us by using graphs. The saying "a picture is worth a thousand words" may explain why graphs are used to convey factual data. A weather report might show the rainfall for the last few months by using a bar graph. The evening news is likely to show the behavior of the Dow Jones Industrial Average by using a line graph. The federal government displays how your taxes are spent by using a pie chart. Even though we might think that graphs should be easier to understand than a table of numbers, we are often confused by them, and we find ourselves skipping over the graph when we read an article.

One reason we have trouble reading graphs is that we do not fully understand how the different parts of a graph are used to help us interpret the information presented. It is important to understand what is meant by the title, labels, and legend of a graph. A graph whose title is "Daily High Temperature for New York City in August" would look different from one whose title is "Average Daily Temperature for New York City in August." The labels of a graph might indicate whether the temperature is measured in degrees Fahrenheit (abbreviated as °F) or degrees Celsius (°C) or whether profits are measured in thousands or millions of dollars. The legend of a graph may state that a solid line represents the number of VCRs sold and that a dotted line represents the number of CD players sold.

We can easily become confused when reading a graph if we fail to recognize that the quantities represented in a graph usually increase as you move from bottom to top and as you move from left to right. For example, a graph of the total rainfall for the month of October might show that the number of inches of rain increases as you move from bottom to top and that time increases as you move from left to right.

We also have difficulty using the scale of a graph to determine the actual quantity represented. For example, if the label of a graph states that sales are measured in thousands of dollars, and the graph shows that sales for February were exactly halfway between 200 and 300, this would mean that February sales were $250,000.

Another difficulty in working with graphs involves applying the notion of a percent to determining the quantity represented in a graph. For example, if a pie chart shows that 15% of the graduating class at a community college are over the age of 35, and there are 640 students in the class, this means that 96 students (640 × 15%) are over the age of 35. If you do not remember what is meant by a percent or how to solve problems using percents, you will not be able to interpret the information presented in many graphs.

Finally, we are often confused by the many different kinds of graphs, and we do not know which kinds of graphs are best for displaying which kinds of information. A line graph could be used to show how the expenditures for a computer company changed over time, but you would need a pie chart to illustrate what percents of the expenditures for a given year were used for personnel, office space, equipment, and supplies.

HINTS FOR STUDYING GRAPHS

When you read a graph, it is very important to pay attention to all the different parts of a graph. The title of a graph and the labels along the horizontal and vertical axes enable you to identify the types of data presented and the quantities represented. The legend or key tells you what each type of bar, line, or symbol represents. When you look at bar graphs, line graphs, and pictograms, notice whether quantities increase as you move upward and to the right. Use the scale of a graph to calculate the actual quantities represented. Refresh your knowledge of percents so that you are able to determine the values represented in a pie chart. Also, become familiar with the differences between bar graphs, pictographs, line graphs, and pie charts; and learn which types of data are best represented by which types of graphs.

BAR GRAPHS IN DAILY LIFE

Bar graphs are named as such because horizontal or vertical bars are drawn to compare different quantities. The size of each bar is proportional to the size of the quantity it represents. Bar graphs are used to represent a limited number of specific quantities. For example, you might use a bar graph to show the number of computers sold by a mail order house each day for a week. This graph would include 7 bars, one for each day. However, it would be impractical to use a bar graph to show the number of computers sold each day for an entire year, since that would require you to draw 365 bars. The **scale** of a bar graph, which is used to determine the quantity represented by each bar, can be determined by looking at the horizontal or vertical axis.

An example of a bar graph is shown in Figure 7.1. The title "Record High Temperatures by Continent in Degrees Fahrenheit" tells you what information you can expect to obtain by reading this graph. For example, you can find out the record high temperature for Europe, but you could not find out the record high temperature for France. The horizontal axis labels indicate the continent that is represented by each bar. The labels on the vertical axis indicate that temperature is measured in degrees Fahrenheit and that each grid line represents a 2° change in temperature. We will now answer a few questions that pertain to this graph.

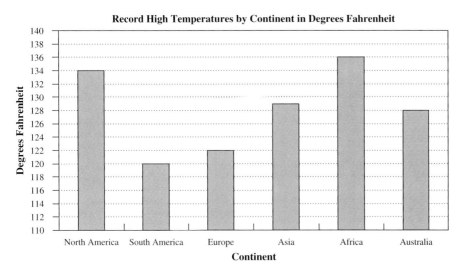

Source: *U.S. Army Corps of Engineers, Engineer Topographic Laboratories.*

Figure 7.1

1. Which continent has the highest record high temperature and what is it?
    Africa has the highest record high temperature of 136°F.
2. Which continent has a record high temperature of 122°F?
    Europe has a record high temperature of 122°F.
3. By how many degrees does the record high temperature of North America exceed that of Australia?

$$
\begin{array}{ll}
134°F & \text{North America} \\
-\ 128°F & \text{Australia} \\
\hline
6°F &
\end{array}
$$

The record high temperature of North America exceeds that of Australia by 6°F.

4. Which two continents had record high temperatures that were most nearly the same, and by how much did they differ?

The record high temperature of Asia (129°F) is most nearly the same as the record high temperature of Australia (128°F), and they differ by 1°F.

PICTOGRAPHS IN DAILY LIFE

Pictographs use repetitive pictures or symbols to represent different quantities. Often pictographs can be used to represent the same information as shown in a bar graph. Since pictographs use pictures instead of bars to compare quantities, they can be more interesting to look at than bar graphs, but they are often less accurate and more difficult to create. The **key** or **legend** of a pictograph tells you the quantity that is represented by each symbol. The larger the number, the more symbols used to display that amount. Sometimes a piece of a symbol is used to depict a fraction of the amount represented by one symbol.

An example of a pictograph showing annual computer sales for various countries is seen in Figure 7.2. The key tells you that each computer symbol represents sales of 10,000 computers. We will now answer a few questions that pertain to this pictograph.

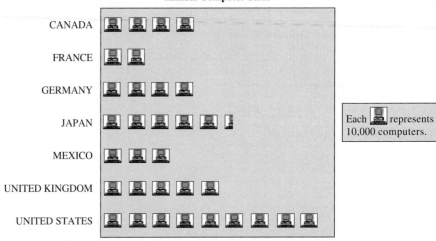

Figure 7.2

1. The greatest number of computers were sold in which country? How many computers were sold in that country?

The greatest number of computers were sold in the United States. Since the United States is followed by 9 computer symbols and each symbol represents 10,000 computers, this means that 90,000 computers were sold in the United States.

2. How many computers were sold in Japan?

    Japan is followed by $5\frac{1}{2}$ computer symbols. Since $5\frac{1}{2} \times 10{,}000 = 55{,}000$, this means that 55,000 computers were sold in Japan.

3. What countries had annual sales of 40,000 computers?

    The countries that had annual sales of 40,000 computers are Canada and Germany, since both are followed by 4 computer symbols.

4. How many more computers were sold in the United Kingdom than in France?

$$
\begin{array}{rl}
50{,}000 & \text{United Kingdom} \\
- \ 20{,}000 & \text{France} \\
\hline
30{,}000 &
\end{array}
$$

So 30,000 more computers were sold in the United Kingdom than in France.

LINE GRAPHS IN DAILY LIFE

Line graphs are used to show trends, and they usually illustrate how something changes over time. A line graph is drawn by first plotting data points that correspond to specific points in time and then connecting those points with a line. Line graphs that have more data points for a specified time period are more accurate, since the lines that connect the points do not represent actual values. Many times, different types of lines, such as solid, dotted, thick, and thin, are drawn on the same graph to enable you to compare trends for different things. The **key** or **legend** tells you which item is represented by each type of line.

An example of a line graph comparing unemployment rates for four countries for a 20-year period is shown in Figure 7.3. The key shows the four different types of lines that are used to depict the unemployment rates for the United States, the United Kingdom, Italy, and Japan. Notice that the data points on the graph tell us the percent of the labor force that is unemployed every 5 years from 1975 to 1995. Therefore, by reading this graph, you can determine the unemployment rate for the United States in 1985, but not in 1983. We will now answer the following questions that pertain to this line graph.

1. Which country had the lowest unemployment rate for the period from 1975 to 1995?

    Japan had the lowest unemployment rate for this period.

2. Which countries had the same unemployment rate in 1990, and what was this rate?

    Both Italy and the United Kingdom had an unemployment rate of 7% in 1990.

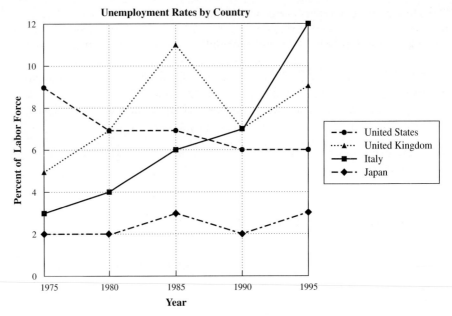

Unemployment Rates by Country

Source: *Bureau of Labor Statistics, U.S. Department of Labor.*

Figure 7.3

3. In what year did the United States have its highest unemployment rate, and what was this rate?

    The United States had its highest unemployment rate in 1975 of 9%.

4. Which country saw the greatest increase in unemployment from 1975 to 1995, and by how much did its unemployment rate change during this period?

    Italy had the greatest increase in unemployment. Its unemployment rate increased from 3% in 1975 to 12% in 1995. Therefore, Italy's unemployment rate increased 9% from 1975 to 1995.

5. Which country showed the sharpest decline in unemployment for a 5-year period, and when did this occur?

    The United Kingdom showed the sharpest decline in unemployment from 1985 to 1990 when the unemployment rate decreased from 11% to 7%.

PIE CHARTS IN DAILY LIFE

Pie charts illustrate how a whole is divided into parts. They are often called **circle graphs,** because a circle is used to represent the whole, and the **sectors** of the circle, which look like pieces of the pie, represent the various parts. The size of each sector is proportional to the amount it represents. Each sector has a label that tells you the part of the whole it represents and the value of that part.

The sum of the quantities represented by each sector must equal the total amount represented by the whole circle. For example, if a pie chart represents how each dollar of tax revenue is spent, and different sectors show how many cents are spent on items such as social security, defense, and human services, then the sum of all the pieces must equal $1.00. Often, each sector of a pie chart represents a percent of the whole, and the sum of all sectors equals 100% or 1 whole pie.

A pie chart showing the leading causes of death in the United States in 1 year is shown in Figure 7.4. Each sector, or piece of the pie, has a label indicating a cause of death and a corresponding percent that indicates the relative number of people who died from that cause. Notice that the sum of the percents represented in all the sectors of the circle is 100%. We will now answer a few questions related to this pie chart.

Leading Causes of Death in the United States

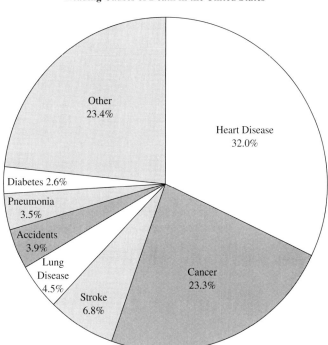

Source: *National Center for Health Statistics, U.S. Department of Health and Human Services.*

Figure 7.4

1. What was the leading cause of death in the year represented by this pie chart?

The leading cause of death was heart disease, because it is represented by the largest sector.

2. What percent of the people who died that year died from causes other than heart disease and cancer?

   Add the percent of people who died from heart disease and the percent of people who died from cancer. Then subtract that percent from 100% to find the remaining percent who died from other causes.

32.0%	Heart disease
+ 23.3%	Cancer
55.3%	Died from heart disease or cancer
100.0%	Total deaths
− 55.3%	Deaths from heart disease and cancer
44.7%	

   Therefore, 44.7% of the people died from causes other than heart disease or cancer.

3. If 2,300,000 people died in the year represented by this graph, how many people died of heart disease?

   To calculate the number of people who died of heart disease, multiply the total number of people who died that year by the percent of those who died of heart disease:

   Total number deaths × % Heart disease deaths = Number of heart disease deaths

   $$2{,}300{,}000 \times 32\% = 2{,}300{,}000 \times 0.32 = 736{,}000 \text{ heart disease deaths}$$

   Therefore, 736,000 people died of heart disease that year.

4. How many more people died from accidents than from diabetes?

   Calculate the total number of deaths from accidents and the total number of deaths from diabetes. Then find the difference between those numbers.

   Total number of deaths × % Accident deaths = Number of accident deaths

   $$2{,}300{,}000 \times 3.9\% = 2{,}300{,}000 \times 0.039 = 89{,}700 \text{ accident deaths}$$

   Total number of deaths × % Diabetes deaths = Number of diabetes deaths

   $$2{,}300{,}000 \times 2.6\% = 2{,}300{,}000 \times 0.026 = 59{,}800 \text{ diabetes deaths}$$

89,700	Accidents
− 59,800	Diabetes
29,900	More deaths from accidents than diabetes

   Therefore, 29,900 more people died from accidents than from diabetes.
   Another way to solve this problem is to first calculate the difference in percentages for deaths by accidents and diabetes and then multiply

that result by 2,300,000:

$$
\begin{array}{ll}
3.9\% & \text{Accidents} \\
\underline{-\;2.6\%} & \text{Diabetes} \\
1.3\% & \text{More deaths from accidents than diabetes}
\end{array}
$$

Total number of deaths $\times$ % More accidents than diabetes

$\qquad\qquad$ = How many more from accidents than from diabetes

$\qquad$ 2,300,000 $\times$ 1.3% = 2,300,000 $\times$ 0.013

$\qquad\qquad$ = 29,900 more from accidents than from diabetes

Therefore, 29,900 more people died from accidents than from diabetes.

5. How many people died from heart disease or strokes?

   Add the percent of people who died from heart disease to the percent of people who died from strokes. Then multiply that total percent by 2,300,000.

$$
\begin{array}{ll}
32.0\% & \text{Heart disease} \\
\underline{+\;6.8\%} & \text{Stroke} \\
38.8\% & \text{Died from heart disease or stroke}
\end{array}
$$

Total number of deaths $\times$ % Heart disease or stroke deaths

$\qquad\qquad$ = Number of heart disease or stroke deaths

$\qquad$ 2,300,000 $\times$ 38.8% = 2,300,000 $\times$ 0.388

$\qquad\qquad$ = 892,400 heart disease or stroke deaths

Therefore, 892,400 people died from heart disease or stroke.

 # STRATEGIES FOR SUCCESS

After seeing examples of the different kinds of graphs and learning how to interpret the information presented in them, you may be less inclined to skip over a graph the next time you see one in a newspaper or magazine. It takes time to read a graph, but it is definitely worth that time if you are able to analyze all the data it contains. Paying close attention to the different parts of a graph, such as the title, labels, and legend, will help you gain an understanding of its overall significance. When you start to read the graph, determine whether quantities increase as your eye moves upward or to the right, and practice using the scale of the graph to calculate the exact values depicted. If you have forgotten how to solve problems using percents, take the time to refresh your knowledge. Percents are especially important in being able to calculate the values represented by pie charts. Finally, try to remember which kinds of graphs are best suited to display which kinds of data. Bar graphs and pictograms are best used to represent a limited number of specific quantities. Pie charts illustrate how a whole is divided into parts. Line graphs are used to show how quantities change over time and often compare trends for related events. Here is a summary of the strategies for getting the most out of graphs.

STRATEGIES FOR SUCCESS WITH GRAPHS

1. Learn how to use the title, labels, and legend of a graph to help you interpret the information presented.

2. Remember that the quantities represented in a graph usually increase as you move from bottom to top and from left to right.

3. Use the scale of a graph to calculate the actual quantities represented by the graph.

4. Review percents, and use them to calculate the values displayed in a graph.

5. Learn which kinds of graphs are best for displaying which kinds of information.

CHAPTER 7 EXERCISES

1. Find two examples of graphs in a magazine, newspaper, or on the Internet. Explain to a friend how to interpret the information displayed in these graphs.

2. Keep track of the high and low temperatures every day for 1 week. Draw a line graph to display these data.

3. Determine how much money you spent last year for various living expenses, such as housing, food, clothing, transportation, and education. Calculate the percent spent on each category, and draw a pie chart to illustrate this.

8

Succeeding with Signed Numbers

 MATH MEMORIES

"I could never do algebra, and I know that's partly because I never under stood what to do with positive and negative numbers."

"All I remember is that two negatives make a positive, but I have no idea what that means."

"I've been embarrassed by my inability to figure out negative numbers, so I avoid them whenever I can."

"I never learned the basics of positive and negative numbers, and to this day it impairs my ability to do basic algebra."

 COMMON PROBLEMS

One of the biggest obstacles making it difficult for people to advance their knowledge of mathematics is their inability to add, subtract, multiply, and divide positive and negative numbers. We often have trouble remembering the rules for performing these operations, because we have tried to memorize what to do, instead of understanding why an operation is done in a particular way. For example, we might remember that "two negatives make a positive," but we don't have a clear idea as to what this really means. Fortunately, once you learn how to work with signed numbers, the calculations are relatively easy.

Since we do not encounter negative numbers a lot in daily living situations, we lack opportunities to practice doing calculations with them, and the techniques we learned in school are easily forgotten. The terminology associated with learning these techniques can also be confusing. Words such as *absolute value* and *opposite* sound simple, but unless we understand the precise meaning of these terms, we cannot follow the procedures that include them. When working with negative numbers, we see lots of minus signs, sometimes two or more in succession, and this confuses us even further. Finally, even if we have mastered the techniques for performing operations on signed numbers, we will have

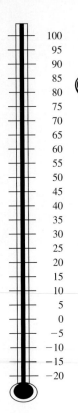

Figure 8.1

difficulty solving problems with positive and negative fractions and decimals unless we can easily perform calculations on positive fractions and decimals.

HINTS FOR STUDYING SIGNED NUMBERS

To gain a basic understanding of the relationship between positive and negative numbers, it is helpful to think of a common example such as temperature.

On a cold winter day, if the temperature is 5 degrees below 0, we could represent this as −5°F (read as "negative five degrees Fahrenheit"). Recall that temperature is measured in degrees on the Fahrenheit scale in the United States. We can see that the number −5 is 5 units below 0 on the thermometer shown in Figure 8.1. The number −5 is the same distance from 0 as the number 5, which is 5 units above 0. The number −5 is said to be the *opposite* of the number 5, because these numbers are on opposite sides of 0, the same distance away.

In mathematics, we often use a number line (instead of a thermometer) to illustrate the relationship between positive and negative numbers, as shown in Figure 8.2.

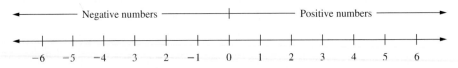

Figure 8.2

The number 0, located at the center of this number line, has no value. It is the reference point from which positive and negative numbers are measured. Positive numbers are greater than 0 (>0) and appear to the right of 0 on a number line. Negative numbers are less than 0 (<0) and appear to the left of 0 on a number line. The number 0 is considered to be neither positive nor negative. Notice that negative numbers are always preceded by a − sign, but positive numbers are usually not preceded by a + sign. We write the number "negative five" as −5, but we write the number "positive five" as 5.

Pairs of numbers on either side of 0 the same distance away are **opposites.** For example, the numbers 3 and −3 are opposites, and the numbers 9 and −9 are opposites. The whole numbers, $0, 1, 2, 3, 4, 5, \cdots$, and their opposites, $-1, -2, -3, -4, -5, \cdots$, are called **integers.** The three dots indicate that the list of integers goes on without end.

The distance between a number and 0 is called its **absolute value.** For example, the absolute value of −8 is 8, since −8 is 8 units from 0 on a number line. We write this as

$$|-8| = 8$$

The vertical bars indicate absolute value. The absolute value of 8 is also 8, since 8 is 8 units from 0 on a number line.

$$|8| = 8$$

The absolute value of any nonzero number is positive, since we measure distance in positive units. The concept of absolute value also applies to fractions and decimals, as shown in these examples:

$$\left|\frac{2}{5}\right| = \left|-\frac{2}{5}\right| = \frac{2}{5}$$

$$|4.7| = |-4.7| = 4.7$$

We can see from these examples that a number and its opposite have the same absolute value, since they are the same distance from zero.

When you are working with signed numbers, it is important to understand that the $-$ sign has three distinct meanings. The first use of the $-$ sign is probably the most familiar to you, and that is to indicate the operation of subtraction, as in the equation $8 - 3 = 5$. The second use of the $-$ sign is to indicate a negative number, such as -6, which is read as "negative six." The third use of the $-$ sign is to indicate the opposite of a number. For example, the expression $-(-4)$ is read as "the opposite of negative four." The first $-$ sign indicates the opposite of the expression in parentheses, and the second $-$ sign indicates a negative number. Since the opposite of a negative number is a positive number, the opposite of negative four is positive four.

$$-(-4) = 4$$
$$\uparrow \quad \uparrow$$

the opposite of   negative four

The next few sections will describe the techniques for adding, subtracting, multiplying, and dividing signed numbers. As you study these procedures, keep in mind a simple example that will help you remember the technique at a later date. If you have trouble performing these four basic operations on positive and negative fractions and decimals, review Chapters 4 and 5 to ensure that you have mastered the skills needed to work with positive fractions and decimals.

ADDITION OF SIGNED NUMBERS

To understand how to add signed numbers, we can think of changes in temperature or can use a number line to illustrate the procedure. For example, if it is 2 degrees below 0 and the temperature drops another 4 degrees, the resulting temperature is 6 degrees below 0.

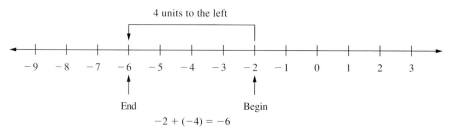

Figure 8.3

Mathematically, this can be represented by the following equation.

$$-2 + (-4) = -6$$

Using the number line shown in Figure 8.3, we begin at -2. To add -4, we then move 4 units to the **left,** since we are adding a **negative** number. We end at the number -6.

Therefore, to add two negative numbers, add their absolute values and put a $-$ sign in front of the result. For example, to add $-12 + (-5)$, we add their absolute values, $12 + 5 = 17$, and put a $-$ sign in front of the result: $-12 + (-5) = -17$. This procedure is summarized here.

To Add Two Negative Numbers

1. Add their absolute values.   **2.** Put a $-$ sign in front of the result.

Consider these examples:

$-31 + (-57) = -88$ Add $31 + 57 = 88$. Put $-$ sign in front.

$-\dfrac{1}{4} + \left(-\dfrac{3}{8}\right) = -\dfrac{2}{8} + \left(-\dfrac{3}{8}\right) = -\dfrac{5}{8}$ Add $\dfrac{2}{8} + \dfrac{3}{8} = \dfrac{5}{8}$. Put $-$ sign in front.

$-6.2 + (-3.4) = -9.6$ Add $6.2 + 3.4 = 9.6$. Put $-$ sign in front.

We can use the same technique to illustrate the procedure for adding a positive number and a negative number. For example, if it is 3 degrees below 0 and the temperature rises 7 degrees, the resulting temperature is 4 degrees above 0. Mathematically, we express this as follows:

$$-3 + 7 = 4$$

Using the number line in Figure 8.4, we begin at -3. To add 7, we move 7 units to the **right** since we are adding a **positive** number. We end at the number 4.

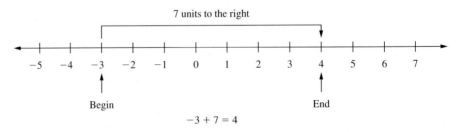

Figure 8.4

The number line shown in Figure 8.5 illustrates another example, 2 + (−9). We begin at 2, move 9 units to the left, and end at −7. Therefore, 2 + (−9) = −7.

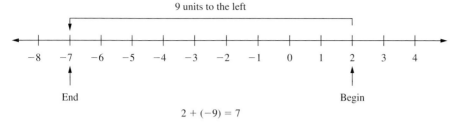

2 + (−9) = 7

Figure 8.5

Notice that to add a positive number and a negative number, we actually first find the difference between the absolute values of the numbers being added. The sign of the answer is the same as that of the number that is farther from zero, that is, the number with the larger absolute value. For example, to add −14 + 6, we first find the absolute values of the two numbers, which are 14 and 6. We then subtract the smaller absolute value from the larger absolute value, which in this case is 14 − 6 = 8. Since −14 is farther from zero than 6 is, and since −14 is negative, the sign of the answer is also negative. Therefore, −14 + 6 = −8. This procedure is summarized here.

To Add a Positive Number and a Negative Number

1. Find the absolute values of the two numbers.
2. Subtract the smaller absolute value from the larger absolute value.

3. The sign of the answer is the same as the sign of the number with the larger absolute value.

For example,

$$-53 + 98 = 45 \qquad \text{Since } 98 - 53 = 45 \text{ and } 98 \text{ is positive}$$

$$\frac{1}{2} + \left(-\frac{5}{8}\right) = \frac{4}{8} + \left(-\frac{5}{8}\right) = -\frac{1}{8} \qquad \text{Since } \frac{5}{8} - \frac{4}{8} = \frac{1}{8} \text{ and } -\frac{5}{8} \text{ is negative}$$

$$-6.9 + 2.7 = -4.2 \qquad \text{Since } 6.9 - 2.7 = 4.2 \text{ and } -6.9 \text{ is negative}$$

SUBTRACTION OF SIGNED NUMBERS

To determine how to subtract positive and negative numbers, let us think about how we subtract positive numbers. We will begin with a problem that we already know how to solve, such as 9 − 2. We know that 9 − 2 = 7. Now that we can add signed numbers, we can rewrite this subtraction problem as an addition problem and get the same answer:

$$9 - 2 = 9 + (-2) = 7$$

This means that subtracting 2 from 9 is the same as adding -2 to 9. The answer is still 7. Therefore, we do not need to learn any additional rules for subtracting signed numbers. We simply rewrite a subtraction problem as an addition problem, and we apply the rules for adding signed numbers.

To Subtract a Signed Number

Add the opposite of the number being subtracted.

Therefore, to subtract a negative number, we add a positive number. For example, to subtract -3 from 8, we add 3.

$$8 - (-3) = 8 + 3 = 11$$

As we solve this problem, we can say to ourselves, "eight **minus** a **negative** three equals eight **plus** a **positive** three equals eleven." To show that subtracting a negative 3 is the same as adding a positive 3, we could have also written this problem as follows:

$$8 - (-3) = 8 + (+3) = 11$$

We usually write positive 3 as simply 3, but if it helps, you may want to show the extra $+$ sign.

Likewise, to subtract a positive number, we add a negative number. For example, to subtract 7 from 5, we add a -7.

$$5 - 7 = 5 + (-7) = -2$$

As we solve this problem, we can say to ourselves, "five **minus** a **positive** seven equals five **plus** a **negative** seven equals negative two."

Here are some additional examples of subtracting signed numbers:

$-13 - (-9) = -13 + 9 = -4$	To subtract -9, add 9.
$42 - 97 = 42 + (-97) = -55$	To subtract 97, add -97.
$-\dfrac{1}{3} - \left(-\dfrac{5}{6}\right) = -\dfrac{1}{3} + \dfrac{5}{6} = -\dfrac{2}{6} + \dfrac{5}{6} = \dfrac{3}{6} = \dfrac{1}{2}$	To subtract $-\dfrac{5}{6}$, add $\dfrac{5}{6}$.
$8.7 - (-2.5) = 8.7 + 2.5 = 11.2$	To subtract -2.5, add 2.5.

Subtraction of signed numbers can be confusing and time-consuming, unless you translate the problem to an addition problem. Once you become familiar with this procedure, you will be able to do this translation from addition to subtraction mentally, and you will not even need to write it down. Also, this technique will make it easier for you to avoid careless mistakes.

MULTIPLICATION OF SIGNED NUMBERS

To understand the rules for multiplying positive and negative numbers, it is helpful to think of what is meant by a negative number. For example, the number -8 means the opposite of 8. It is also the result obtained when the number 8 is multiplied by -1.

$$-1 \cdot 8 = -8$$

We often use parentheses to indicate the operation of multiplication when working with signed numbers.

$$(-1)(8) = -8$$

Notice that in this example, we multiplied a negative number and a positive number, and the result was a negative number. We also obtain a negative number when we multiply a positive number and a negative number.

$$(4)(-6) = -24$$

Multiplying a positive number and a negative number results in a negative number.

For example,

$$(-9)(5) = -45$$
$$\left(\frac{4}{5}\right)\left(-\frac{2}{3}\right) = -\frac{8}{15}$$
$$(-2.1)(4) = -8.4$$

We will now look at what is meant by the opposite of a negative number, in order to come up with a rule for multiplying two negative numbers. Recall that the expression $-(-5)$ is read as "the opposite of negative five," which is 5.

$$-(-5) = 5$$

We could rewrite this expression as the product of -1 and -5.

$$(-1)(-5) = 5$$

We have therefore illustrated the following:

Multiplying two negative numbers results in a positive number.

For example,

$$(-7)(-3) = 21$$

$$\left(-\frac{5}{6}\right)\left(-\frac{1}{8}\right) = \frac{5}{48}$$

$$(-6.2)(-8) = 49.6$$

Since the product of two negative numbers is a positive number, it is some-times said that "two negatives make a positive."

We can derive the rules for multiplying any number of signed numbers by multiplying two numbers at a time to arrive at a solution. For example, let us see what happens when we multiply three negative numbers.

$$(-5)(-2)(-4)$$
$$= \quad (10) \quad (-4)$$
$$= \quad\quad -40$$

Notice that the product of *three* negative numbers is *negative*.

We will now multiply four negative numbers.

$$(-3)(-4)(-2)(-5)$$
$$= \quad (12) \quad\quad (10)$$
$$= \quad\quad 120$$

Therefore, the product of *four* negative numbers is *positive*.

Let's now multiply five negative numbers.

$$(-2)(-4)(-1)(-5)(-7)$$
$$= \quad (8) \quad\quad (5) \quad (-7)$$
$$= \quad\quad (40) \quad\quad (-7)$$
$$= \quad\quad\quad -280$$

We can see that the product of *five* negative numbers is *negative*.

Finally, we will multiply six negative numbers.

$$(-5)(-4)(-2)(-3)(-5)(-10)$$
$$= \quad (20) \quad\quad (6) \quad\quad (50)$$
$$= \quad\quad (120) \quad\quad\quad (50)$$
$$= \quad\quad\quad 6{,}000$$

Therefore, the product of *six* negative numbers is *positive*.

These examples show that when we multiply signed numbers, if one, three, or five of the numbers are negative, the result (or product) is a negative number. If we multiply two, four, or six negative numbers, the product is a positive number. Therefore, the following is true.

The product of an **odd** number of negative numbers is a **negative** number.
The product of an **even** number of negative numbers is a **positive** number.

DIVISION OF SIGNED NUMBERS

We can apply the rules for multiplying signed numbers to dividing signed numbers, since division is the same as multiplying by the reciprocal. For example, when you divide a positive number by a negative number or when you divide a negative number by a positive number, the result (or quotient) is a negative number.

$$-63 \div 7 = (-63)\left(\frac{1}{7}\right) = \ ^-9$$

$$42 \div (-6) = (42)\left(-\frac{1}{6}\right) = -7$$

We have therefore shown the following.

Dividing two numbers of opposite sign results in a negative number.

For example,

$$-32 \div 4 = -8$$

$$5.6 \div (-0.8) = -7$$

$$-\frac{3}{8} \div \frac{2}{5} = -\frac{3}{8} \times \frac{5}{2} = -\frac{15}{16}$$

Likewise, when we divide two negative numbers, the result (or quotient) is positive. For example,

$$-72 \div (-8) = (-72)\left(-\frac{1}{8}\right) = 9$$

$$-\frac{5}{12} \div \left(-\frac{2}{3}\right) = \left(-\frac{5}{12}\right)\left(-\frac{3}{2}\right) = \frac{15}{24} = \frac{5}{8}$$

Therefore,

Dividing two negative numbers results in a positive number.

For example,

$$-60 \div (-12) = 5$$
$$-7.2 \div (-9) = 0.8$$

Another type of problem related to multiplying and dividing signed numbers involves simplifying a fraction in which signed numbers are multiplied in the numerator and denominator. Consider the following fraction:

$$\frac{(-15)(4)}{(-6)(-18)}$$

To simplify this fraction, we first determine the sign of the answer. Since there are three negative numbers being multiplied and divided, the result is negative. We then reduce the fraction to lowest terms, ignoring the signs of the individual numbers.

$$\frac{(-15)(4)}{(-6)(-18)} = -\frac{(15)(4)}{(6)(18)} = -\frac{\overset{5}{\cancel{15}})(\overset{2}{\cancel{4}})}{(\underset{3}{\cancel{6}})(\underset{\underset{3}{6}}{\cancel{18}})} = -\frac{5}{9}$$

SIGNED NUMBERS IN DAILY LIFE: BANK ACCOUNT BALANCE

We will now use our knowledge of signed numbers to solve a few word problems. An accountant has overdrawn his bank account by $71.54. How much money must he deposit to bring his balance up to $425? To solve this problem, we can find the difference between the new balance of $425 and the current balance of −$71.54. We use a negative balance, −$71.54, to indicate that the account is overdrawn.

$$425 - (-71.54) \qquad 425.00$$
$$= 425 + 71.54 \qquad \underline{+\ 71.54}$$
$$= 496.54 \qquad\qquad 496.54$$

Therefore, the accountant must deposit $496.54.

SIGNED NUMBERS IN DAILY LIFE: ELEVATION

Here is another example using positive and negative numbers. The highest point in Africa, Mount Kilimanjaro, is 19,911 feet higher than the lowest point in Africa, Lake Assal, which is 571 feet below sea level. What is the elevation of Mount Kilimanjaro? To solve this problem, we add 19,911 to −571. We use a negative number to represent the fact that Lake Assal is 571 feet *below* sea level.

$$-571 + 19{,}911 \qquad 19{,}911$$
$$= 19{,}911 + (-571) \qquad -\ \underline{\ \ 571}$$
$$= 19{,}340 \qquad\qquad 19{,}340$$

Therefore, Mount Kilimanjaro has an elevation of 19,340 feet.

STRATEGIES FOR SUCCESS

By now, you may be starting to think that working with signed numbers is not as difficult as you had originally thought. However, you still might be afraid that if you forget the rules, you will be just as intimidated by negative numbers as you were before you read this chapter. Whenever you need to add signed numbers, just think of a simple example, such as a change in temperature, or visualize a number line. This will help you remember what to do. Don't forget that to subtract a signed number, you simply add its opposite. If you need to multiply or divide signed numbers, remember that if there are an *odd* number of negative factors, the result is *negative;* and if there are an *even* number of negative factors, the result is *positive*. Finally, if you have trouble working with positive and negative fractions and decimals, try to do the same operation with positive and negative integers. If you succeed, you simply need to review fractions and decimals. Here is a summary of the strategies that can help you succeed with signed numbers.

STRATEGIES FOR SUCCESS WITH SIGNED NUMBERS

1. Think of a simple example to help you remember the rules for adding, subtracting, multiplying, and dividing signed numbers.

2. Keep in mind practical examples of negative numbers, such as temperature, an overdrawn bank account, or elevation below sea level.

3. Learn the meaning of terms such as *absolute value* and *opposite*.

4. Remember that a − sign can represent a negative number, the operation subtraction, or the opposite of a number.

5. Review the techniques for working with positive fractions and decimals if you are having difficulty with positive and negative fractions and decimals.

CHAPTER 8 EXERCISES

1. Explain in your own words how you would add two signed numbers. Include one example using a positive and a negative number and another using two negative numbers.

2. Explain in your own words two different uses of the "−" sign, and give examples of each.

3. Use the Internet or an almanac to find the highest and lowest temperatures recorded in the United States during last year. Calculate the difference between those two temperatures. Calculate the average of those two temperatures.

4. What operations do you find the easiest and hardest to do with signed numbers? Explain why.

CHAPTER

Mastering Measurement

MATH MEMORIES

"As an undergraduate, I avoided math like the Black Plague. But now that I am studying to be a fashion designer, I need to know how to measure fabric for the clothes I design."

"Anytime I need to do home improvements, I am frustrated by my lack of skill in math because I cannot figure out how much carpeting I need or how much paint I should buy."

"I always loved science, but I was afraid to go further with it because I was weak in math and could not understand the metric system."

COMMON PROBLEMS

In our society, we rely heavily on standards of measurement so that we can assign numerical values to the properties of things we need to compare. We need different types of measurement to indicate the value of different properties. For example, we might measure the duration of a math class in minutes, the height of a child in inches, the weight of a turkey in pounds, the volume of gasoline in gallons, and the temperature outside in degrees Fahrenheit.

Even though we constantly see examples of measurement in daily life, we are often confused by the fact that the same property may be assigned different values, depending on the standard used. The different standards are called **units of measurement,** and they indicate the value of a known quantity. For example, time might be measured in seconds, minutes, hours, days, weeks, months, or years. We need different units of measurement to measure quantities having large differences in magnitude. For example, we might measure the time needed to bake cookies in minutes, but the age of a person in years.

Another reason why measurement is so confusing is that we do not remember how to convert from one unit of measurement to another. If we knew that a class lasted 45 minutes and someone told us instead that the class would last $\frac{3}{4}$ hour, we would not know that this was the same amount of time unless we knew that 60 minutes = 1 hour. Also, it is difficult for us to work with fractional units of measurement if we do not remember the techniques for performing operations on fractions.

Even though a quantity such as time is measured by using the same standards throughout the world, the quantities of length, weight, volume, and temperature can be measured by using two different systems, the English system and the metric system. Although the English system is used primarily in the United States and the metric system is used throughout the rest of the world, we are beginning to see more and more examples of the metric system in this country. If we are unsure of the relationship between pints and fluid ounces for measuring volume, we will probably be even more confused when we see that a can of soda contains 12 fl oz (fluid ounces) or 355 ml (milliliters).

Another source of confusion is that units of measurement are almost always represented by using their abbreviations. We are probably very familiar with the fact that "in." is the abbreviation for inches and "mi" is the abbreviation for miles, but we might not know that "fl oz" is the abbreviation for fluid ounces, or that "ml" is the abbreviation for milliliters.

We also have a lot of difficulty converting from one form of measurement to another, especially when the units are unfamiliar to us. If we know that 12 inches = 1 foot and we are asked to convert 2 feet to inches, we might be able to reason that we should multiply by 12 because feet are larger than inches. However, when we are confronted by units of measurement that are unfamiliar to us, our intuition cannot be relied upon, and we resort to making a guess as to whether we need to multiply or divide. Finally, we are often totally dumbfounded when we need to do conversions that involve more than two units of measurement, such as converting from pints to gallons, or from days to minutes.

HINTS FOR STUDYING MEASUREMENT

One way to gain confidence in working with measurement is to learn the most common equivalent units of measurement associated with length, weight, volume, and time. It is not necessary to memorize all the conversion facts, but knowing those that we encounter frequently, such as 12 inches = 1 foot, 16 ounces = 1 pound, and 4 quarts = 1 gallon, will make it easier for you to work with converting units of measurement. Also, when you learn equivalent values for different units of measurement, learn their abbreviations as well. Even more important than learning the conversion facts is to learn the standard technique for converting from one unit of measurement to another. If you forget a conversion fact, you can always look it up; but if you cannot remember whether to multiply or divide when converting from one unit to another, you have a 50% chance of making the wrong guess. Also, knowing a standard technique will enable you to easily do conversions, especially for problems that involve working with more than two different units of measurement. If you have difficulty remembering the technique, think of a simple example for which you already know the answer, to help refresh your memory. To acquire greater skill in working with the metric system, learn the meaning of the different metric prefixes. In addition, if you have difficulty understanding the relationship between English and metric units of measurement, learn approximate equivalents for the same quantity in both systems, such as the fact that 1 quart ≈ 1 liter. This will enable you to estimate conversions from one system to another.

This chapter includes many tables that summarize equivalent units of measurement for time, length, weight, and volume. Do not feel overwhelmed by all this information. These tables are simply a reference guide to make it easy for you to look up conversion facts that you may not remember.

UNITS OF TIME

We will begin with the most common entity we measure throughout each and every day, which is time. Units of time are very familiar to all of us, since we use them so frequently. The following table is a summary of equivalent units of time, with the abbreviation for each unit given in parentheses.

Equivalent Units of Time
1 minute (min) = 60 seconds (sec)
1 hour (hr) = 60 minutes (min)
1 day (da) = 24 hours (hr)
1 week (wk) = 7 days (da)
1 year (yr) = 12 months (mo)
1 year (yr) = 365 days (da)

Since you probably already know all the conversion factors listed, you can focus your attention on learning the method we will use to convert from one unit of time to another. When units of measurement are very familiar to us, such as those associated with time, it is very easy to figure out how to convert from one unit to another. For example, to convert 3 hours to minutes, we would multiply: 3 × 60. To convert 30 months to years, we would divide: 30 ÷ 12. However, when the units of measurement are unfamiliar to you, often you resort to guessing what to do. We will now introduce a conversion technique that will not require you to know whether you need to multiply or divide. This involves multiplying the quantity to be converted by an appropriate unit fraction.

A **unit fraction** is a fraction equivalent to 1. You use equivalent units of measurement to create a unit fraction. For example, the following fractions are all examples of unit fractions.

$$\frac{1 \text{ min}}{60 \text{ sec}} \qquad \text{since } 1 \text{ min} = 60 \text{ sec}$$

$$\frac{24 \text{ hr}}{1 \text{ da}} \qquad \text{since } 24 \text{ hr} = 1 \text{ da}$$

$$\frac{12 \text{ mo}}{1 \text{ yr}} \qquad \text{since } 12 \text{ mo} = 1 \text{ yr}$$

Notice that in each case, the numerator and denominator both represent the same quantity. Therefore, all unit fractions equal the number 1.

$$\frac{1 \text{ min}}{60 \text{ sec}} = \frac{1 \text{ min}}{1 \text{ min}} = 1$$

To convert 3 hours to minutes using this technique, we multiply 3 hours by a unit fraction that has the unit we want to convert **to** (min) in the **numerator** and the unit we want to convert **from** (hr) in the **denominator.** This unit fraction is $\frac{60 \text{ min}}{1 \text{ hr}}$. Therefore, to convert 3 hours to minutes, we multiply $3 \text{ hr} \times \frac{60 \text{ min}}{1 \text{ hr}}$. Notice that since we have the unit of hours in both the numerator and the denominator, we can cancel out the hours, just as we do when we have the same number or factor in the numerator and denominator.

$$3 \text{ hr} = 3 \text{ hr} \times \frac{60 \text{ min}}{1 \text{ hr}} = 3 \text{ hr} \times \frac{60 \text{ min}}{1 \text{ hr}} = 180 \text{ min}$$

Therefore, 3 hours is equal to 180 minutes. This procedure for converting units of measurement by multiplying by unit fractions is called **dimensional analysis.** The word *dimension* refers to something that can be measured and the units used to express that quantity. For example, time is measured in units such as hours and minutes. Length is measured in units such as feet and inches. The technique we just used to convert units of measurement is summarized here.

To Convert Units of Measurement

1. Find a unit fraction that has the unit to be converted *to* in the numerator and the unit to be converted *from* in the denominator.

2. Multiply the quantity to be converted by this unit fraction.

To convert 30 months to years using this technique, we first find a unit fraction with years in the numerator and months in the denominator, which is $\dfrac{1 \text{ yr}}{12 \text{ mo}}$. We then multiply 30 months by this unit fraction as follows:

$$30 \text{ mo} = 30 \text{ mo} \times \frac{1 \text{ yr}}{12 \text{ mo}} = \frac{\overset{5}{\cancel{30} \text{ mo}}}{1} \times \frac{1 \text{ yr}}{\underset{2}{\cancel{12} \text{ mo}}} = \frac{5}{2} \text{ yr} = 2\frac{1}{2} \text{ yr}$$

Therefore, 30 months is equal to $2\dfrac{1}{2}$ years.

UNITS OF LENGTH

We will now use this technique to convert from one unit of length to another. We will first work with units in the English system, which are used extensively in the United States. Be certain to memorize the conversion factors presented in the following table, along with the abbreviations for the common units of length.

Equivalent Units of Length
1 foot (ft) = 12 inches (in.)
1 yard (yd) = 3 feet (ft)
1 mile (mi) = 5,280 feet (ft)

Let us now solve the following problem. An airplane en route to Cleveland is flying at a cruising altitude of 31,680 feet. How many miles above the earth is the airplane flying? To solve this problem, we need to convert 31,680 feet to miles. We first need to find a unit fraction with miles in the numerator and feet in the denominator, which is $\dfrac{1 \text{ mi}}{5{,}280 \text{ ft}}$. We then multiply 31,680 feet by this unit fraction as follows:

$$31{,}680 \text{ ft} = 31{,}680 \text{ ft} \times \frac{1 \text{ mi}}{5{,}280 \text{ ft}} = 31{,}680 \text{ \cancel{ft}} \times \frac{1 \text{ mi}}{5{,}280 \text{ \cancel{ft}}} = \frac{31{,}680}{5{,}280} \text{ mi}$$

$$= \frac{3{,}168}{528} \text{ mi} = \frac{528}{88} \text{ mi} = \frac{66}{11} \text{ mi} = 6 \text{ mi}$$

Therefore, the airplane is flying 6 miles above the earth.

We will now look at a more difficult problem that requires us to do a multistep conversion. For example, let us convert $\dfrac{1}{8}$ mile to inches. We can do this conversion in two steps, by first converting miles to feet and then converting feet to inches. We convert $\frac{1}{8}$ mile to feet by multiplying $\frac{1}{8}$ mile by a unit fraction with feet in the numerator and miles in the denominator, as follows:

$$\frac{1}{8} \text{ mi} = \frac{1}{8} \text{ mi} \times \frac{5{,}280 \text{ ft}}{1 \text{ mi}} = \frac{1}{8} \text{ m\!i} \times \frac{5{,}280 \text{ ft}}{1 \text{ m\!i}} = \frac{5{,}280}{8} \text{ ft} = 660 \text{ ft}$$

We then convert 660 feet to inches by multiplying 660 feet by a unit fraction with inches in the numerator and feet in the denominator.

$$660 \text{ ft} = 660 \text{ ft} \times \frac{12 \text{ in.}}{1 \text{ ft}} = 660 \text{ f\!t} \times \frac{12 \text{ in.}}{1 \text{ f\!t}} = 7{,}920 \text{ in.}$$

Therefore, $\frac{1}{8}$ mile is equal to 7,920 inches.

We could also convert $\frac{1}{8}$ mile to inches in one step by multiplying $\frac{1}{8}$ mile by two unit fractions, the first having miles in the denominator and the second having inches in the numerator.

$$\frac{1}{8} \text{ mi} = \frac{1}{8} \text{ mi} \times \frac{5{,}280 \text{ ft}}{1 \text{ mi}} \times \frac{12 \text{ in.}}{1 \text{ ft}} = \frac{1}{\overset{}{\underset{1}{8}}} \text{ m\!i} \times \frac{\overset{660}{5{,}280} \text{ f\!t}}{1 \text{ m\!i}} \times \frac{12 \text{ in.}}{1 \text{ f\!t}} = 7{,}920 \text{ in.}$$

Notice that the units of miles and feet cancel, and we obtain the same result, that $\frac{1}{8}$ mile is equal to 7,920 inches.

UNITS OF WEIGHT

The following table, which summarizes equivalent units of weight in the English system, probably contains information that is also familiar to you. Be sure to learn these conversion facts and the abbreviations for the common units of weight.

Equivalent Units of Weight
1 pound (lb) = 16 ounces (oz)
1 ton (ton) = 2,000 pounds (lb)

Let us now solve the following problem. A piece of Swiss cheese weighs $1\frac{3}{4}$ pounds, and a piece of cheddar cheese weighs 25 ounces. Which weighs more, the Swiss cheese or the cheddar cheese? To compare these weights, they must be expressed in the same units of measurement. Therefore we must convert either $1\frac{3}{4}$ pounds to ounces or 25 ounces to pounds. Let us convert $1\frac{3}{4}$ pounds to ounces by multiplying $1\frac{3}{4}$ pounds by a unit fraction with ounces in the numerator and pounds in the denominator.

$$1\frac{3}{4}\text{ lb} = 1\frac{3}{4}\text{ lb} \times \frac{16\text{ oz}}{1\text{ lb}} = 1\frac{3}{4}\cancel{\text{lb}} \times \frac{16\text{ oz}}{1\cancel{\text{lb}}} = \frac{7}{4} \times \frac{16}{1}\text{ oz} = \frac{7 \times \overset{4}{\cancel{16}}}{\underset{1}{\cancel{4}}}\text{ oz} = 28\text{ oz}$$

Therefore, the Swiss cheese weighs 28 ounces. Since the cheddar cheese weighs 25 ounces, the Swiss cheese weighs 3 ounces more than the cheddar cheese.

UNITS OF VOLUME

The equivalent units of volume in the English system are summarized in the following table. Many conversion factors such as those for converting cups to pints or quarts to gallons are probably very familiar to you. You may need to learn others, such as those for converting fluid ounces to pints.

Equivalent Units of Volume
1 pint (pt) = 2 cups (c)
1 quart (qt) = 2 pints (pt)
1 gallon (gal) = 4 quarts (qt)
1 pint (pt) = 16 fluid ounces (fl oz)
1 tablespoon (tbsp) = $\frac{1}{2}$ fluid ounce (fl oz)
1 tablespoon (tbsp) = 3 teaspoons (tsp)

We will now use the information presented in this table to solve the following problem, which involves working with conversion factors that may be new to you. How many tablespoons are in a pint? This is similar to the problem we solved earlier that involved multiple units of measurement, in which we converted $\frac{1}{8}$ mile to inches. To solve this problem, we need to convert first from pints to fluid ounces and then from fluid ounces to tablespoons. We can therefore multiply 1 pint by two unit fractions, the first having fluid ounces in the numerator and pints in the denominator and the second having tablespoons in the numerator and fluid ounces in the denominator.

$$1\text{ pt} = 1\text{ pt} \times \frac{16\text{ fl oz}}{1\text{ pt}} \times \frac{1\text{ tbsp}}{\frac{1}{2}\text{ fl oz}} = 1\cancel{\text{pt}} \times \frac{16\cancel{\text{fl oz}}}{1\cancel{\text{pt}}} \times \frac{1\text{ tbsp}}{\frac{1}{2}\cancel{\text{fl oz}}} = \frac{16}{\frac{1}{2}}\text{ tbsp}$$

$$= 16 \times 2\text{ tbsp} = 32\text{ tbsp}$$

Therefore, 1 pint is equal to 32 tablespoons.

THE METRIC SYSTEM

The metric system is the system of measurement used in most countries outside the United States. The basic units of measurement in the metric system along with their abbreviations are given in the following table.

Basic Metric Units of Measurement
Length: meter (m)   Weight: gram (g)   Capacity: liter (l)

A meter is a little more than a yard. A gram is about equal to $\frac{1}{30}$ ounce. A liter is equivalent to a little more than a quart. In the metric system, equivalent units of measurement are derived by multiplying or dividing the standard units of measurement by powers of 10. The relative size of the metric unit of measurement is indicated by the metric prefixes, listed in the following table with their abbreviations.

Metric Prefixes
milli (m)—thousandth $\left(\frac{1}{1,000}\right)$ centi (c)—hundredth $\left(\frac{1}{100}\right)$ deci (d)—tenth $\left(\frac{1}{10}\right)$ deka (da)—ten (10)   hecto (h)—hundred (100)   kilo (k)—thousand (1,000)

We attach a metric prefix to a basic metric unit to obtain different units of measurement. We will illustrate this procedure with the following examples:

1. What metric unit of weight is equivalent to 1000 grams?
    Since the metric prefix for grams is *kilo,* 1 kilogram (kg) = 1,000 grams (g).

2. What metric unit of length is equivalent to $\frac{1}{100}$ meter?

    Since the metric prefix for $\frac{1}{100}$ is *centi,* 1 centimeter (cm) = $\frac{1}{100}$ meter (m).

3. What metric unit of volume is equivalent to $\frac{1}{1,000}$ liter?

    Since the metric prefix for $\frac{1}{1,000}$ is *milli,* 1 milliliter (ml) = $\frac{1}{1,000}$ liter.

4. What metric unit of length is equivalent to 100 meters?

Since the metric prefix for 100 is *hecto,* 1 hectometer (hm) = 100 meters (m).

We convert from one unit of measurement to another in the metric system in the same way as we do in the English system. That is, we multiply by a unit fraction that has the unit we are converting *to* in the numerator and the unit we are converting *from* in the denominator. Since the metric system is based on powers of 10, the arithmetic is simpler than converting English units of measurement. For example, to convert 800 meters to kilometers, we multiply 800 meters by a unit fraction that has kilometers in the numerator and meters in the denominator. Since kilo means 1,000, 1 kilometer (km) = 1,000 meters (m), and this unit fraction is $\frac{1 \text{ km}}{1,000 \text{ m}}$.

$$800 \text{ m} = 800 \text{ m} \times \frac{1 \text{ km}}{1,000 \text{ m}} = 800 \text{ m} \times \frac{1 \text{ km}}{1,000 \text{ m}} = \frac{800}{1,000} \text{ km} = 0.8 \text{ km}$$

Therefore, 800 meters = 0.8 kilometer.

ESTIMATING CONVERSIONS BETWEEN ENGLISH AND METRIC UNITS

Since we encounter situations in our daily lives in which quantities are measured in both English and metric units, it is important to be able to convert between the two systems. In most situations, just knowing how to estimate conversions between English and metric units will greatly enhance your ability to "think metric." The following table summarizes approximations for converting between English and metric units of length, weight, and volume.

Length Approximations
1 meter (m) ≈ 1 yard (yd)
1 inch (in.) ≈ $2\frac{1}{2}$ centimeters (cm)
1 kilometer (km) ≈ $\frac{5}{8}$ mile (mi)

Weight Approximations
1 ounce (oz) ≈ 30 grams (g)
1 kilogram (kg) ≈ 2.2 pounds (lb)
1 ton (ton) ≈ 1 metric ton (t)

Volume Approximations
1 quart (qt) ≈ 1 liter (l)
1 fluid ounce (fl oz) ≈ 30 milliliters (ml)
1 teaspoon (tsp) ≈ 5 milliliters (ml)
1 tablespoon (tbsp) ≈ 15 milliliters (ml)

We will now use the information presented in this table to solve the following problems. A can of soda contains 12 fluid ounces. Approximately how many milliliters does the can contain? To convert fluid ounces to milliliters, multiply 12 fluid ounces by a unit fraction that has milliliters in the numerator and fluid ounces in the denominator. Since 1 fluid ounce ≈ 30 milliliters, this unit fraction is $\dfrac{30 \text{ ml}}{1 \text{ fl oz}}$.

$$12 \text{ fl oz} \approx 12 \text{ fl oz} \times \frac{30 \text{ ml}}{1 \text{ fl oz}} = 12 \,\cancel{\text{fl oz}} \times \frac{30 \text{ ml}}{1 \,\cancel{\text{fl oz}}} = 360 \text{ ml}$$

Therefore, a can of soda contains about 360 milliliters.

A road race is 10 kilometers long. Approximately how many miles long is the race? To convert kilometers to miles, multiply by a unit fraction that has miles in the numerator and kilometers in the denominator. Since 1 kilometer ≈ $\dfrac{5}{8}$ mile, this unit fraction is $\dfrac{\frac{5}{8} \text{ mi}}{1 \text{ km}}$.

$$10 \text{ km} \approx 10 \text{ km} \times \frac{\frac{5}{8} \text{ mi}}{1 \text{ km}} = 10 \,\cancel{\text{km}} \times \frac{\frac{5}{8} \text{ mi}}{1 \,\cancel{\text{km}}} = 10 \times \frac{5}{8} \text{ mi} = \frac{50}{8} \text{ mi} = \frac{25}{4} \text{ mi} = 6\frac{1}{4} \text{ mi}$$

Therefore, the race is about $6\frac{1}{4}$ miles long.

MEASUREMENT IN DAILY LIFE: UNIT PRICE

One of the most common examples of measurement is determining which size of a product is the best buy. This requires us to find the **unit price** of each item, which is the price per 1 unit of measurement. If the sizes of the items to be compared are not expressed in the same units of measurement, we must first convert them to the same unit of measurement before calculating their unit prices. The item with the smallest unit price is considered to be the best buy. Consider this example. A 2.5-pound box of laundry detergent sells for $3.88, and a 50-ounce box of the same product sells for $4.95. Which size is the better buy? To solve this problem, we first need to convert 2.5 pounds to ounces or 50 ounces to pounds, so that both boxes are expressed in the same units of measurement. Let us convert 2.5 pounds to ounces.

$$2.5 \text{ lb} = 2.5 \text{ lb} \times \frac{16 \text{ oz}}{1 \text{ lb}} = 2.5 \,\cancel{\text{lb}} \times \frac{16 \text{ oz}}{1 \,\cancel{\text{lb}}} = 40 \text{ oz}$$

Therefore, 2.5 pounds is equal to 40 ounces. To calculate the unit prices, we divide the price of each box by its weight in ounces.

Unit price of 2.5-lb or 40-oz box: $\dfrac{\$3.88}{40\ oz} = \$0.097/oz$

Unit price of 50-oz box: $\dfrac{\$4.95}{50\ oz} = \$0.099/oz$

Since the 40-ounce or 2.5-pound box has the smaller unit price, it is less expensive. Therefore, the 2.5-pound box at $3.88 is the better buy.

STRATEGIES FOR SUCCESS

Now that you have seen a number of problems that require you to convert from one unit of measurement to another, you can appreciate the importance of knowing the common equivalent units of measurement and the abbreviations for those units. To avoid confusion when you convert from one unit of measurement to another, use the standard technique of multiplying by a unit fraction that has the unit to be converted *to* in the numerator and the unit to be converted *from* in the denominator. Also, reviewing the procedures for multiplying, dividing, and reducing fractions will give you added confidence in doing conversions. To become familiar with the metric system, remember that the meter, gram, and liter are the standard units of length, weight, and volume. Also, learn the meaning of the metric prefixes and how they can be used to determine equivalent units of measurement in the metric system. Finally, to enhance your ability to "think metric," learn the common approximate conversion factors for converting between English and metric units. You might even want to practice estimating conversions between the English and metric units that appear on the labels of items you see in the grocery store. Here is a summary of the strategies we have discussed for mastering measurement.

STRATEGIES FOR SUCCESS WITH MEASUREMENT

1. Learn the most common equivalent units of measurement associated with time, length, weight, and volume.
2. Learn the abbreviations for units of measurement.
3. To convert from one unit of measurement to another, multiply by the appropriate unit fraction.
4. Review the procedures for working with fractions.
5. Learn the standard metric units of measurement and the meaning of the metric prefixes.
6. Learn the approximate conversion factors for converting between English and metric units.

CHAPTER 9 EXERCISES

1. Guess the approximate height of this math book in inches. Then measure it to determine the exact height. How close was your guess?

2. Guess the approximate diameter of a quarter in millimeters. Then measure it to determine the exact value. How close was your guess?

3. How many days have passed since you were born? How many hours have passed since you were born? How did you calculate your answers?

4. How many miles are there from where you live to where you work or attend school? Estimate this distance in feet and then determine the exact answer. Explain how you arrived at your estimate and how you calculated the exact distance in feet.

10

Grasping Geometry

MATH MEMORIES

"I hate geometry. It makes my head hurt."

"I could never get geometry because you had to remember all these complicated formulas which never made sense to me. I'd panic whenever I had to solve a problem, and my mind would just go blank."

"I was always poor at math, especially geometry. But now I need to take the GREs and I need to know geometry to get a good score."

"Geometry seemed like a foreign language to me because I never understood how the numbers and letters were related."

"The first class I ever failed was geometry, and I was devastated."

COMMON PROBLEMS

Geometry is one of the more interesting areas of mathematics because it deals directly with the measurement of physical objects in the world. We need geometry to figure out how long a fence is needed to enclose a backyard, how much carpeting is needed to cover a living room floor, or how much water is needed to fill a swimming pool. However, many of us find geometry very confusing, and we avoid using it to solve problems that occur in daily living situations. One reason for this is that we are confused by the terminology used in geometry. We do not remember the names of the various geometric figures or the meaning of the words used to describe their properties. Another reason is that we do not understand the relationship between geometric properties of perimeter, area, and volume and how they are measured using linear, square, and cubic units of measurement. If we are not familiar with the procedure for converting from one unit of measurement to another, we will not be able to work with geometric figures whose dimensions are expressed in different units. Geometry may seem difficult to you because you also have trouble remembering the formulas used to calculate the perimeter, area, and volume of various geometric figures. If you are not familiar with algebraic notation, working with formulas that contain both letters and numbers will seem very intimidating. Since solving geometric problems requires us to be able to combine a variety of skills, we often feel as though we do not know where to begin, and our lack of progress can leave us confused and frustrated.

HINTS FOR STUDYING GEOMETRY

When you are learning geometry, it is important that you begin by learning the names of the various geometric figures and the terminology used to describe their properties. Often, looking at a picture will help you remember the characteristics of a geometric figure, including the dimensions used to describe it. It is also important that you understand the relationship between linear units, square units, and cubic units of measurement. Perimeter is measured in linear units, such as feet. Area is measured in square units, such as square feet. Volume is measured in cubic units, such as cubic feet. If you have forgotten the technique for converting from one unit of measurement to another, review the material presented in Chapter 9.

We will be introducing a variety of formulas in this chapter, to enable you to calculate the perimeter, area, or volume of various geometric figures. A **formula** is an equation that states how to calculate an unknown quantity, given other known quantities. For example, if we know the dimensions of a rectangle, that is, its length and width, we can use a formula to calculate its area.

Whenever possible, try to understand how formulas are derived, because this will help you to remember them. Geometry will seem easier to you if you memorize the formulas for calculating the geometric properties of common figures. Write the formulas you have trouble remembering on index cards or Post-It notes, and put them in a location you look at frequently, such as your refrigerator door or bathroom mirror. You may find that you learn them in no time. Since formulas include a combination of letters and numbers, you need to understand what each letter represents in order to use them correctly. Once you have practiced solving lots of problems that require you to use formulas, you will be more confident in working with the algebraic notation used in formulas.

Finally, if you do not know where to begin in solving a geometry problem, start by writing down what you *do* know about the problem. This may include drawing a picture, listing the dimensions of the object, or writing down the formula needed to solve the problem.

This chapter includes a lot of formulas, which are the most common ones learned in geometry. You may vaguely remember many of these from prior mathematics courses, and just seeing them again may raise your anxiety level. It may take some time to become familiar with them, and it may not even be necessary for you to learn all these formulas at this time. Just keep in mind that they are all included here so that you can look them up when you need them.

PERIMETER

Perimeter is a measurement of the distance around an object. Since distance has only one dimension—length, we measure perimeter by using linear units of measurement. As an example, suppose a farmer wanted to enclose the field shown in Figure 10.1 with a fence. How many yards of fencing would she need?

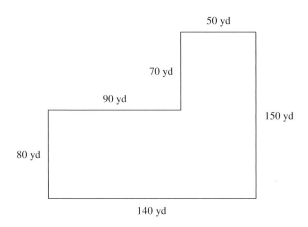

Figure 10.1

To solve this problem, we need to find the perimeter, or the distance around the field. To do this, we simply add the lengths of the sides.

$$\text{Perimeter} = 50 + 150 + 140 + 80 + 90 + 70$$
$$= 580$$

Therefore, the farmer needs 580 yards of fencing to enclose the field.

We can represent this procedure for finding the perimeter by using a formula, which is actually nothing more than a shorthand notation. A formula for finding the perimeter of a figure with six sides could be written as follows:

$$P = s_1 + s_2 + s_3 + s_4 + s_5 + s_6$$

In this formula, P represents the perimeter; s_1, which is read as "s sub one," represents the length of the first side; s_2, which is read as "s sub two," represents the length of the second side; s_3 represents the length of the third side; and so on. Sometimes, we may refer to this as the formula for finding the perimeter of a six-sided polygon. A **polygon** is a figure with many sides.

Some of the more common polygons include a triangle, rectangle, and square. A **triangle** is a polygon that has three sides. A **rectangle** is a figure with four sides that meet in a right angle. A **right angle** is formed when a vertical line and a horizontal line meet. A **square** is a type of rectangle, whose sides are all equal. A picture of a rectangle is shown in Figure 10.2.

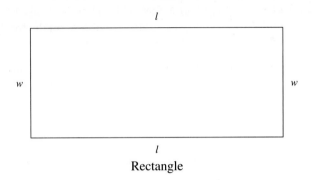

Rectangle

Figure 10.2

We now illustrate how to derive the formula for finding the perimeter of a rectangle. The dimensions of a rectangle are its length, which is represented by the letter l, and its width, which is represented by the letter w. To find the perimeter of the rectangle shown in Figure 10.2, we can simply add the four sides.

$$P = l + w + l + w$$
$$= l + l + w + w$$
$$= 2l + 2w$$

It is important to note that $l + l$ is the same as $2 \times l$ or $2l$, and $w + w$ is the same as $2 \times w$ or $2w$. In algebra, there are many ways to indicate that a number, or constant, is multiplied by a letter or variable. For example, we can indicate that the constant 2 is multiplied by variable w in any of the following ways:

$$2 \times w = 2 \cdot w = 2w$$

Therefore, whenever you see a constant and a variable next to each other with no symbol between them, it is assumed that the operation to be performed is multiplication.

Here is a summary of the formulas we have discussed for finding the perimeter.

Perimeter Formulas
Polygon with sides s_1, s_2, s_3, s_4, . . . :
$P = s_1 + s_2 + s_3 + s_4 + \cdots$
Rectangle with length l and width w:
$P = 2l + 2w$

GEOMETRY IN DAILY LIFE: PERIMETER

The following example illustrates an application of the perimeter. A restaurant owner wants to place a string of lights along the border of his restaurant window that measures 9 feet long and 6 feet wide. How long must the string of lights be? To solve this problem, we will use the formula for finding the perimeter of a rectangle with $l = 9$ feet and $w = 6$ feet.

$$P = 2l + 2w$$
$$= 2(9) + 2(6)$$
$$= 18 + 12$$
$$= 30 \text{ ft}$$

Therefore, the string of lights must be 30 feet long.

AREA

Area is a measurement of the surface covered by an object. Since area represents a two-dimensional region, it is measured using square units of measurement. To demonstrate how we might find the area of an object, let us consider the following example.

A hallway is 12 feet long by 6 feet wide. If the floor of the hallway is to be replaced with square tiles that measure 1 foot on each side, how many tiles are needed to cover the floor? To solve this problem, we are asked to determine how many square tiles are needed to cover a rectangular area that is 12 feet in length and 6 feet in width. We begin by drawing a diagram to illustrate the problem, which is shown in Figure 10.3.

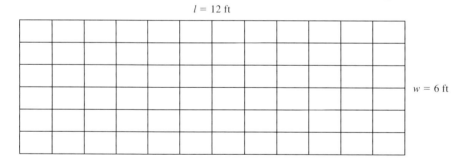

Figure 10.3

Looking at the diagram, we can see that the number of tiles can be calculated by multiplying the length of the hallway by its width. Since $12 \times 6 = 72$, it will take 72 tiles to cover the floor.

By saying that the floor can be covered by 72 tiles that measure 1 foot by 1 foot, we are expressing a way to represent the area of the floor. However, it is more practical to measure the area of an object by using square units of measurement, rather than tiles. Since each of the tiles measures 1 foot on each side, we can say that each tile represents 1 square foot (abbreviated as 1 ft^2). Therefore, 72 tiles represent an area of 72 square feet.

This problem, therefore, illustrates that the procedure for finding the area of a rectangular region is to multiply the length by the width. If we let A represent the area of a rectangle, l represent the length, and w represent the width, then we can represent the area of a rectangle by using the following formula.

$$A = l \times w$$

Using this formula, we can calculate the area of the hallway with $l = 12$ feet and $w = 6$ feet as follows:

$$A = l \times w$$
$$= 12 \text{ ft} \times 6 \text{ ft}$$
$$= 12 \times 6 \times \text{ft} \times \text{ft}$$
$$= 72 \text{ ft}^2$$

Therefore, the area of the hallway is 72 square feet, which is abbreviated as 72 ft^2 or 72 sq ft. Recall that an expression such as 5^2, which is read as "five squared" or "five to the second power," means that 5 is used as a factor 2 times. That is,

$$5^2 = 5 \times 5 = 25$$

Similarly, the expression ft^2 is read as "square feet" and is equal to ft $\times$ ft.

Another geometric figure whose formula for area is similar to that of a rectangle is a parallelogram. A **parallelogram** is a four-sided figure whose opposite sides are parallel. In fact, a rectangle is actually a kind of parallelogram whose sides meet in a right angle. A parallelogram has two dimensions, base b and height h, as illustrated in Figure 10.4.

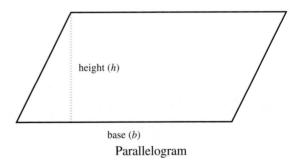

Parallelogram

Figure 10.4

We can see from this diagram that if we cut off the triangular piece on the left side of the parallelogram and attach it to the right side of the figure, we would have a rectangle with length b and width h. Since the area of a rectangle is length times width, the area of this parallelogram is $b \times h$. Therefore, we can use the following formula to find the area of a parallelogram of base b and height h.

$$A = b \cdot h$$

We will now illustrate how to derive the formula for the area of a triangle. A triangle has two dimensions, base b and height h, as illustrated in Figure 10.5. We can see from this diagram that the area of this triangle is actually one-half of the area of a parallelogram of base b and height h. Therefore, we can use the following formula to find the area of a triangle of base b and height h.

$$A = \frac{1}{2}bh$$

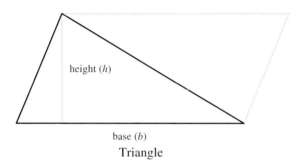

height (h)

base (b)

Triangle

Figure 10.5

Here is a summary of the formulas we have discussed for finding the areas of various figures.

Area Formulas
Rectangle with length l and width w:
$A = l \times w$
Parallelogram with base b and height h:
$A = b \cdot h$
Triangle with base b and height h:
$A = \frac{1}{2}bh$

GEOMETRY IN DAILY LIFE: AREA

Let us now apply our knowledge of area to solving the following problem. How many gallons of paint are needed to paint the ceiling of a lecture hall that is 40 feet long and 15 feet wide, if 1 gallon covers 400 square feet? To solve this problem, we first need to find the area of the ceiling in square feet. Since the ceiling is in the shape of a rectangle, with $l = 40$ ft and $w = 15$ ft, we can find its area as follows:

$$A = l \times w$$
$$= (40 \text{ ft})(15 \text{ ft})$$
$$= 600 \text{ ft}^2$$

We now divide 600 square feet by the area covered by 1 gallon of paint, which is 400 square feet, to find the number of gallons needed to paint the ceiling.

$$600 \text{ ft}^2 \div 400 \text{ ft}^2/\text{gal} = \frac{600 \text{ ft}^2}{400 \text{ ft}^2/\text{gal}} = \frac{600 \text{ ft}^2}{400 \text{ ft}^2/\text{gal}} = \frac{600}{400} \text{gal} = \frac{3}{2} \text{gal} = 1\frac{1}{2}\text{gal}$$

Therefore, $1\frac{1}{2}$ gallons of paint are needed to paint the ceiling.

CIRCLES

A **circle** is a two-dimensional figure whose every point is the same distance away from a fixed point called the **center.** The distance from the center of the circle to its edge is called the **radius** r. The distance along a line that passes through the center from one edge of a circle to another is called the **diameter** d. You can see from the circle illustrated in Figure 10.6 that the diameter of a circle is equal to twice its radius.

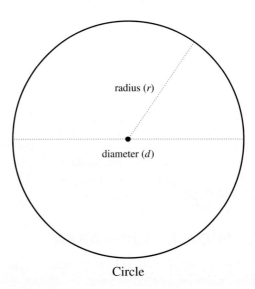

radius (r)

diameter (d)

Circle

Figure 10.6

The **circumference** of a circle is the distance around a circle, or its perimeter. We will now examine the relationship between the circumference of a circle and its diameter. To do this, we measured the circumference and diameter of a few common objects and listed the results in the table that follows. For each object, using a pocket calculator, we then divided the circumference by the diameter, rounded off the result to the nearest ten-thousandth, and recorded the result in this table.

Object	Circumference	Diameter	Circumference / Diameter
Lamp shade	56.5 in.	18 in.	3.1389
Pot	33 in.	10.5 in.	3.1429
Cup	23 cm	7.3 cm	3.1507
Quarter	7.5 cm	2.4 cm	3.1250

Notice that for each object, the result obtained when we divided the circumference by the diameter was a number approximately equal to 3. In fact, the Greeks performed a similar experiment, using measuring devices that were far more precise than the ones we used. They found that the number obtained by dividing the circumference of a circle by its diameter was always exactly equal to the decimal 3.14159265 $\cdots$. The three dots indicate that the division can be carried out indefinitely and will never result in a remainder of 0. The number obtained whenever the circumference of a circle is divided by its diameter is called **pi.** It is represented by the symbol π, the Greek letter pi, and is approximately equal to the decimal 3.14 or the fraction $\frac{22}{7}$. Therefore, if we let C represent the circumference of a circle and let d represent its diameter, the following is true.

$$\frac{C}{d} = \pi$$

If we multiply both sides of this equation by d, we obtain the following formula for the circumference of a circle with diameter d.

$$C = \pi d$$

Since the diameter is equal to 2 times the radius, we can also use this formula to find the circumference of a circle of radius r.

$$C = \pi 2r$$
$$= 2\pi r$$

We will now demonstrate a way to find the area of a circle. Figure 10.7 illustrates a circle with radius r and circumference C that is divided into six pieces, which are called *sectors*.

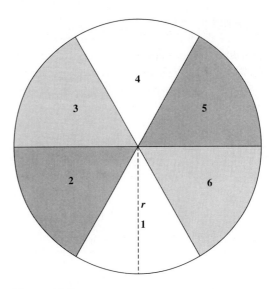

Figure 10.7

If these six sectors are separated and then put back together in the arrangement shown in Figure 10.8, we have a figure that resembles a parallelogram. Notice that the base of the parallelogram is equal to one-half of the circumference $\left(b = \dfrac{1}{2}C\right)$, since the entire circumference forms the top and bottom of the parallelogram. The height of the parallelogram is equal to the radius of the circle ($h = r$).

Since exactly the same pieces that made up the circle in Figure 10.7 were used to create the parallelogram in Figure 10.8, the area of the parallelogram is exactly equal to the area of the circle. To find the area of this parallelogram,

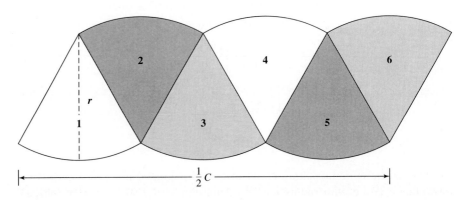

Figure 10.8

we can use the formula $A = bh$ and substitute the values $\frac{1}{2}C$ for b and r for h. Since the circumference of a circle is $2\pi r$, we will then substitute the value $2\pi r$ for C. The result is the formula for the area of a circle with radius r.

$$A = bh$$

$$= \frac{1}{2}Cr \qquad \text{Substitute } b = \frac{1}{2}C \text{ and } h = r.$$

$$= \frac{1}{2}2\pi r \cdot r \qquad \text{Substitute } C = 2\pi r.$$

$$= \pi r^2 \qquad \text{Since } r \cdot r = r^2.$$

Here is a summary of the formulas we have discussed for finding the circumference and area of a circle.

Circle Formulas

Circumference of circle with radius r and diameter d:

$C = 2\pi r \qquad$ or $\qquad C = \pi d$

Area of circle with radius r:

$A = \pi r^2$

GEOMETRY IN DAILY LIFE: CIRCLES

Let us now look at a problem that requires us to apply our knowledge of circles. A snow fence surrounds a circular skating rink that has a diameter of 50 feet. What is the length of the snow fence? Use $\pi \approx 3.14$. Since the length of the fence is the distance around the circular skating rink, we need to find the circumference of a circle with $d = 50$ feet. Substituting into the formula for circumference, we obtain the following:

$$C = \pi d$$
$$= (3.14)(50 \text{ ft})$$
$$= 157 \text{ ft}$$

Therefore, the snow fence is 157 feet long. Remember that since circumference represents a distance, it is expressed in linear units of measurement.

VOLUME

Volume is a measurement of the space enclosed by an object. Since volume is a characteristic of three-dimensional space, it is measured in cubic units of measurement. One way to measure volume is to think about the number of blocks needed to fill a space. Each block would be in the shape of a cube. A **cube** is a three-dimensional figure that has the same length, width, and height. As an example, let us use a block that measures 1 inch on each side as our unit of measurement. This cube, illustrated in Figure 10.9, is said to have a volume of 1 cubic inch, which can be abbreviated as 1 cu in. or 1 in.^{3}.

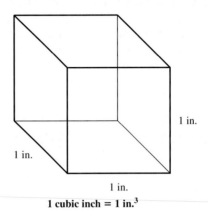

1 in.

1 in.

1 in.

1 cubic inch = 1 in.^{3}

Figure 10.9

Let us now find the volume of an aquarium, in the shape of a rectangular box, that has a length *l* of 20 inches, a width *w* of 10 inches, and a height *h* of 12 inches. One way to determine this is to figure out how many blocks of 1 cubic inch are needed to completely fill the aquarium. Looking at Figure 10.10, we can see that the aquarium is composed of 12 layers of blocks, each 1 inch high.

Therefore, to determine the number of blocks needed to fill the aquarium, we first find the number of blocks needed to cover the bottom layer, and we then multiply that result by the number of layers. Since the bottom layer has

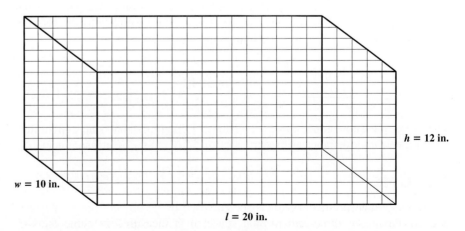

h = 12 in.

w = 10 in.

l = 20 in.

Figure 10.10

20 blocks along its length and 10 blocks along its width, we need 20 × 10 blocks, or 200 blocks, to cover the bottom layer. Since there are 200 blocks in each layer and the aquarium has 12 layers, we need 200 × 12 blocks, or 2,400 blocks, to fill the aquarium. We can also say that the aquarium has a volume of 2,400 cubic inches, since each block measures 1 cubic inch. Note that the technique we used to find the volume is actually the same as that for finding the area of the base $l \times w$ and multiplying that result by the height h.

We have therefore demonstrated that to find the volume V of a rectangular box having length l, width w, and height h, we can simply multiply its length by its width by its height.

$$V = l \times w \times h \qquad \text{or} \qquad V = lwh$$

Remember that if no symbol appears between two letters or between a number and a letter in a formula, it is assumed that they are to be multiplied. Using this formula to find the volume of the aquarium with length 20 inches, width 10 inches, and height 12 inches, we also obtain a volume of 2,400 cubic inches.

$$
\begin{aligned}
V &= l \times w \times h \\
&= (20 \text{ in.})(10 \text{ in.})(12 \text{ in.}) \\
&= (20)(10)(12)(\text{in.})(\text{in.})(\text{in.}) \\
&= 2{,}400 \text{ in.}^3
\end{aligned}
$$

Recall that an expression such as 2^3, which is read as "two cubed" or "two to the third power," means that 2 is used as a factor 3 times. That is,

$$2^3 = 2 \times 2 \times 2 = 8$$

Similarly, the expression in.^{3} is read as "cubic inches" and is equal to in. × in. × in.

Suppose we are also asked to determine how many gallons of water, rounded off to the nearest gallon, are needed to fill this aquarium, given that 1 gallon ≈ 231 cubic inches. To calculate this, we need to convert 2,400 cubic inches to gallons. We therefore multiply 2,400 cubic inches by a unit fraction that has gallons in the numerator and cubic inches in the denominator, as follows:

$$
\begin{aligned}
2{,}400 \text{ in.}^3 \approx 2{,}400 \text{ in.}^3 \times \frac{1 \text{ gal}}{231 \text{ in.}^3} &= 2{,}400 \, \cancel{\text{in.}^3} \times \frac{1 \text{ gal}}{231 \, \cancel{\text{in.}^3}} \\
&= \frac{2{,}400}{231} \text{gal} \approx 10.4 \text{ gal}
\end{aligned}
$$

Since 10.4 ≈ 10, it will take 10 gallons of water to fill this aquarium.

Since a cube is a type of rectangular box, we can also find its volume by multiplying its length by its width by its height. We can let the letter s represent each of the three dimensions of a cube, since its length, width, and height are all the same. Therefore, the formula for the volume V of a cube having side s is as follows:

$$V = l \times w \times h$$
$$= s \times s \times s$$
$$= s^3$$

We will now find the volume of another three-dimensional figure called a cylinder. A **cylinder** is a figure that has two circular bases joined by parallel sides. The distance from the center to the edge of the base is called the **radius,** and the distance between the two bases is called the **height.** A common object in the shape of a cylinder is a can. A cylinder having a base radius r and height h is shown in Figure 10.11.

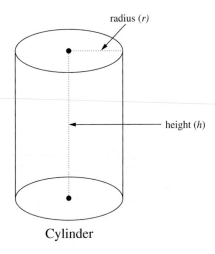

radius (r)

height (h)

Cylinder

Figure 10.11

To find the volume of a cylinder, we can use the same technique that we used to find the volume of the rectangular box, that is, to find the area of the bottom base and multiply that result by the height. Since the base of a cylinder is a circle with radius r, its area is πr^2. Multiplying this by the height h, we obtain $\pi r^2 h$. Therefore, the formula for the volume of a cylinder is

$$V = \pi r^2 h$$

We will now present formulas for finding the volumes of two more solid figures—a cone and a sphere. Since these formulas are derived by using a more advanced branch of mathematics called calculus, we will not attempt to show how these formulas are obtained.

A **cone** is a three-dimensional figure with a circular base whose sides meet in a point called the **apex.** The distance from the center to the edge of the base is called the **radius,** and the distance from the base to the apex is called the **height.** Common objects in the shape of a cone include a funnel and an ice cream cone. A cone having a base radius r and height h is shown in Figure 10.12.

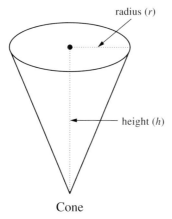

Cone

Figure 10.12

The formula for finding the volume of a cone is as follows:

$$V = \frac{1}{3}\pi r^2 h$$

Since the volume of a cylinder is $\pi r^2 h$, the formula for the volume of a cone makes sense because it states that the volume of a cone is one-third the volume of a cylinder with the same radius and height.

A **sphere** is a three-dimensional figure whose every point is the same distance away from a fixed point called the **center.** The distance from the center of the sphere to any point on its surface is called the **radius.** A ball is an example of an object shaped as a sphere. A sphere with a radius of r is illustrated in Figure 10.13.

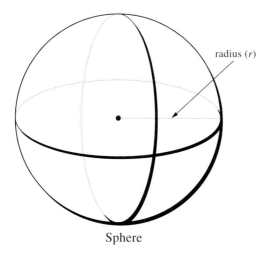

Sphere

Figure 10.13

The formula for finding the volume of a sphere with radius r is

$$V = \frac{4}{3}\pi r^3$$

Here is a summary of the formulas we have discussed for finding the volumes of various solid figures:

Volume Formulas
Cube with side s: $V = s^3$
Rectangular box with length l, width w, and height h: $V = lwh$
Cylinder with radius r and height h: $V = \pi r^2 h$
Cone with radius r and height h: $V = \frac{1}{3}\pi r^2 h$
Sphere with radius r: $V = \frac{4}{3}\pi r^3$

GEOMETRY IN DAILY LIFE: VOLUME

We will now apply our knowledge of volume to solving the following problem. A cylindrical can has a diameter of 4 inches and a height of 7 inches. How many fluid ounces of tomato juice are needed to fill the can if 1 cubic inch is approximately equal to 0.554 fluid ounce? Use $\frac{22}{7}$ as an approximation for π. Since the radius of a circle is equal to one-half of the diameter, the radius of this can is 2 inches. We will first calculate the volume of a cylinder with $r = 2$ inches and $h = 7$ inches.

$$V = \pi r^2 h$$

$$= \frac{22}{7}(2 \text{ in.})^2 (7 \text{ in.})$$

$$= \frac{22}{7}(2 \text{ in.})(2 \text{ in.})(7 \text{ in.})$$

$$= \frac{22}{7}(2)(2)(7)\,(\text{in.})(\text{in.})(\text{in.})$$

$$= \frac{(22)(2)(2)(7)}{7}\,\text{in.}^3$$

$$= \frac{(22)(2)(2)(\cancel{7})}{\cancel{7}} \text{ in.}^3$$
$$= (22)(4) \text{ in.}^3$$
$$= 88 \text{ in.}^3$$

Since 1 cubic inch $\approx$ 0.554 fluid ounce, we will now convert 88 cubic inches to fluid ounces by multiplying by a unit fraction that has fluid ounces in the numerator and cubic inches in the denominator.

$$88 \text{ in.}^3 \approx 88 \text{ in.}^3 \times \frac{0.554 \text{ fl oz}}{1 \text{ in.}^3} = 88 \cancel{\text{ in.}^3} \times \frac{0.554 \text{ fl oz}}{1 \cancel{\text{ in.}^3}}$$
$$= 88 \times 0.554 \text{ fl oz} = 48.752 \text{ fl oz}$$

It will therefore take 48.752 fluid ounces of tomato juice to fill the can.

STRATEGIES FOR SUCCESS

Now that you have seen diagrams of the common geometric figures, it may be easier to remember their names and the dimensions used to describe them. Keep in mind that perimeter is a measurement of distance and is expressed in linear units; area is a measurement of a two-dimensional region and is described using square units; and volume is a measurement of three-dimensional space and is expressed in cubic units. If you have forgotten how to convert from one unit of measurement to another, review the technique for multiplying by a unit fraction that has the unit to be converted *to* in the *numerator* and the unit to be converted *from* in the *denominator*. Be certain to memorize the formulas for calculating the perimeter, area, and volume of common geometric figures. Understanding how some of these formulas were obtained may assist you in memorizing them. Practice solving lots of problems that require you to work with formulas, so that you will become comfortable with algebraic notation. Finally, if you are confused by word problems involving geometry, it may help to draw a diagram of the figure, identify its dimensions, or write down a formula that can be used to solve it. Here is a summary of the strategies that can help you grasp geometry.

STRATEGIES FOR SUCCESS WITH GEOMETRY

1. Learn the names of common geometric figures and their characteristics.

2. When you are solving a problem, determine whether the answer should be expressed in linear, square, or cubic units of measurement.

3. Review the procedure for converting between different units of measurement.

4. Memorize common formulas for calculating the perimeter, area, and volume.

5. Be certain that you understand the meaning of the algebraic notation used in working with formulas.

6. Remember that it may be easier to solve a geometry problem if you draw a diagram, list the figure's dimensions, or write down a formula.

CHAPTER 10 EXERCISES

1. Find the area of the floor of a room where you live, work, or go to school. Make an estimate before you calculate the final answer.

2. Explain the differences between the perimeter, area, and volume, using an example of each.

3. Measure the circumference and diameter of any circular object, using the same units of measurement, and write down those numbers. Divide the circumference by the diameter. What value do you obtain, and what is its significance?

CHAPTER

11

Moving Beyond Math Anxiety

 ## MATH MEMORIES

"Somehow I landed a great job in the financial industry, and now I really want to go to business school. I am sick of being scared of math and sick of being envious of people who can do math."

"I began full of nervousness and trepidation, and now I have a wonderful strength and confidence that I am not stupid. I just need to practice, practice, practice."

"I now realize that I don't have to be afraid of math, and I don't have to feel bad when I make a mistake."

"Now I know that I am capable of 'getting' math. I have a positive outlook and more confidence in my ability to understand it."

"When I fully understand what I am doing, math is a lot of fun and I actually enjoy it."

TAKING THE NEXT STEP

If you have just finished reading the past 10 chapters, you may be feeling a bit overwhelmed by all the mathematics that has been presented. This is quite natural. In fact, if you think that you have mastered all that has been presented simply by reading this book, you probably did not need to read this book at all.

No one would expect to be able to give a piano recital at Carnegie Hall just by reading a book on how to play the piano. It takes years and years of practice for almost anyone to become proficient at playing a musical instrument. Similarly, you cannot expect yourself to be an expert in mathematics just by reading a book on mathematics. It will also take time and practice. Learning math is a lot like learning a foreign language. Reading the material in a textbook can get you started, but until you spend a lot of time speaking and reading the language, you will not become fluent. Likewise, by doing lots of math problems, you will gradually develop proficiency in mathematics.

As you begin to practice doing math, it is very important that you do not become discouraged by mistakes. If you find that you are making lots of mistakes, you may simply be going too fast. If you are an inexperienced driver, when you drive fast, you are more likely to have an accident. However, expert race car drivers can drive very fast without a problem. Once you build up your level of experience, then you can do math more quickly.

It is very important that you take the time to find the right circumstances to enable you to learn math. For many people, the best approach is to simply take a class. However, every math instructor has a different style of teaching, and the pace of a math class can vary widely depending upon how much material must be covered. If you find that your instructor is too confusing or too intimidating, you may need to study math with a different teacher. Many outstanding mathematicians do not have the skills needed to help someone learn math who is struggling with the most basic concepts. If the class moves too quickly, take another course that covers less material over a longer time. If you feel a lot of stress because you are afraid of getting a bad grade, consider taking a noncredit math course. Many students who encounter problems in a math course are quick to blame themselves for their difficulties, and they do not take the steps needed to find the right environment where they can be successful. You need to take charge of your own education and remain confident that you are indeed capable of learning mathematics.

It is essential that you ask lots and lots of questions until you are certain that you fully understand what you are trying to learn. Don't be afraid to ask for help. Most math instructors welcome questions from students; so if you become confused in the middle of a class, ask for further explanation. There is no such thing as a "dumb question," and other students will probably be grateful to you for having the courage to ask a question about something they also did not understand. If the class is moving too fast for you, but the instructor needs to keep moving forward, make a note to remind yourself to ask for help regarding that topic after class. There are often a variety of resources available to you for this purpose, including the instructor's office hours, math labs, and tutoring services.

The critical ingredient to success in mathematics (and anything else) is *practice, practice, practice.* Watching someone else work out a math problem, even if you understand every step, is not the same as being able to do it yourself. You would never expect to be a great musician just by attending a concert, or to be a great athlete just by watching the Olympics, or to be a great painter just by observing an artist at work. In most fields, including music, athletics, and art, there is a big difference between those who have perfected their craft and those who have not. Therefore, after every math class or tutoring session, you need to spend lots of time working out problems on your own, to gain skill and confidence.

Before you begin to solve a math problem, try to estimate the final answer. This will help you catch obvious errors in your calculations. Don't underestimate the value of estimation. In many instances where you use math in daily life, such as in figuring out a tip, a good estimate is so close to the exact answer that it is not necessary to do the actual calculation. Acquiring skill in estimation is just as important as learning how to apply various mathematical techniques.

Finally, it is important to pay attention to things you find enjoyable about doing math. If we focus on our failures and difficulties, we will never develop the confidence or motivation needed to progress. Don't force yourself to do math when you feel tired, distracted, or frustrated. Try to create a positive learning environment for yourself, and set aside time to study when you feel awake, focused, and relaxed. If you succeed in getting the right answer the first time you attempt a problem, take time to acknowledge your success since it will motivate you to keep going further. If you feel frustrated while trying to work through a difficult problem, try an easier one to build your confidence. Take pride in the times when you are able to help your children do their math homework, or figure out the tip when you go out to dinner. As with anything else, the greater joy we experience while working to achieve our goals, the greater desire we will have to pursue our dreams.

STRATEGIES FOR SUCCESS

Here is a summary of the concluding strategies we have discussed in this chapter to help you conquer math anxiety.

STRATEGIES FOR SUCCESS IN CONQUERING MATH ANXIETY

1. Set realistic goals for yourself, and don't expect to quickly become a math expert.
2. Regard mistakes as part of the learning process instead of as obstacles.
3. Learn in your own way, at your own pace.
4. Ask lots of questions and don't be afraid to ask for help.
5. Practice, practice, practice.
6. Don't underestimate the value of estimation.
7. Notice times when you find joy in doing math.

CHAPTER 11 EXERCISES

1. Describe at least two positive experiences you have recently had while learning math. In each case, what steps did you take to ensure your success?
2. How have your study habits changed in trying to learn mathematics since you started reading this book? What changes have you found to be most helpful?
3. Write down at least three suggestions for someone who wants to overcome his or her anxiety about learning math.
4. What goals would you like to achieve during the next 5 years that will require you to increase your proficiency in mathematics? Write down the steps you are planning to take to achieve them.

INDEX